Trees of Righteousness

Fulfillment of the Curses of Deuteronomy 28

Empress Em Sharon Yisrael

Copyright © 2017 Revised Edition 2019 by Empress Em' Sharon Yisrael

Revised Edition. All rights reserved. No part of this publication may be reproduced, distributed, or transmitted in any form or by any means, including photocopying, recording, or other electronic or mechanical methods, without the prior written permission of the publisher, except in the case of brief quotations embodied in critical reviews and certain other noncommercial uses permitted by copyright law.

ISBN: 978-1-7336754-3-7

Liberation's Publishing LLC
West Point, Mississippi
www.liberationspublishing.com

Scripture quotations marked (KJV) matches the 1987 printing. The KJV is in the public domain in the United States.

Scriptures quoted from the Apocrypha match the King James Version. Authorized, 1611.

Copyright © 2011 by Common English Bible

Dedication

This book is dedicated to the Twelve Tribes of Israel that are scattered throughout the earth. It is my hope that we find ourselves as "The Hidden Ones" the true Children of Israel.

"The Holy Martyrs of Sevaste"

Empress Em Sharon Yisrael

Table of Contents

Forward vii

Introduction 1

Jacob's Trouble 5

Who Am I? 17

Who Are We? 39

The Flood 49

The Place Pineal 55

Northern Kingdom vs. Southern Kingdom 61

Transatlantic Slave Trade 75

Arab Slavery 79

Christianity 101

Daddy, God's Love for Us 107

Conclusion 119

Photocopies of Historic Artwork 131

Forward

To all Hebrew Israelites who have awakened and found out who you are, I am grateful to our heavenly father that light (knowledge) has come to you. I have been instructed to use the Greek name of Jesus by our heavenly father. God allowed his Word (the bible), to go out into the four corners of the earth in the King James Version. Jesus is a stone of stumbling and a rock of offence, a rock that makes them fall, 1 Peter 2:8.

We are not familiar with the Hebrew names of God and Jesus. I am to use the knowledge that people already know of God, Jesus, the Holy Spirit or Ghost. The whole world is familiar with the King James Version of the bible. The entire world knows the name of Jesus. Our father wants me to use what we already have, so that your learning of who we are will not be confusing or hard to grasp. If we are to wake up as a people, it has to be done with knowledge that we can all identify with, and b lack people who are in the churches today know Jesus.

The apocryphal books that were last printed in 1611 were a part of the King James Bible. These apocryphal books are our credentials that identify us as the Children of Israel descendants. That is why they were removed from the bible. They have now re-surfaced to aid us in self-discovery. So, in Jesus name, which is the King's "language", I write this book, that enlightenment will come to all of the twelve tribes of Israel.

Introduction

I have only been sent to Israel to inform, to instruct, and to wake up our people. This is not about the world: They are the true Gentiles. This is a self-discovery of who the Africans of the Diaspora are. A story that has never been told to this degree but will stand in the light of truth. This story includes our restoration.

This is the story of those descendant from slavery, the exiled Hebrew's story. It tells what has happened to us while being scattered worldwide, while exiled from our homeland. It reveals what was stolen from us, who we are, why we fell, and our near future exodus. If we don't know who we are, then we won't know where we are going. Our heavenly Father has planned a phenomenal redemption from the curses/punishment over our lives. We have an awesome date with destiny!

This book is named Trees of Righteousness, Isa. 61:3, because we are Zion, "The Hidden Ones" hidden in plain sight. This is all spiritual. Daddy God says, it's not by power, nor by might, but by my spirit says the Lord, Zechariah 4:6. You don't have to work for it, and you certainly cannot purchase it. It comes to his children by faith and because Daddy God loves us and desires to gives us the best. Daddy God will give us beauty for ashes, the oil of joy for mourning, a garment of praise for the spirit of heaviness that we may be called 'Trees of Righteousness'; the planting of the Lord, that he may be glorified.

Empress Em Sharon Yisrael

The Most High God (Daddy) has sent me as a Mother to Israel to make his children aware of our near future return home. I am his representative of the Kingdom of Heaven in the earth realm. He has made me an Empress, Em Sharon Yisrael, a teacher, and Gatherer. He has called me to go before the leaders of the world, to decree and declare to them, to give everything back that was stolen from the Children of Shem, which will fulfill Isa. 60:5. He is on his way back with his hosts of angelic armies to defend and reclaim us. He has called me to gather the remnant of the 144,000 Children of Israel which will be left worldwide as a result of the race war that we still must face in this end time age of Gentile rule, Rev. 7. In Isa. 45:3 he says, "And I will give thee the treasures of darkness, and hidden riches of secret places, that thou mayest know that I, the Lord, which call thee by thy name, am the God of Israel.

Take a look at the treasures in secret places that he gave me to show everyone. They show our true legacy that has been left to us for redemption. These are the times we are entering into. Daddy's word says there is nothing covered that shall not be revealed, neither hid that shall not be known, Luke 12:2. 2019 is our year of release from the 400-year curse of Deut. 28:15-68/Gen 15:13-14/Acts 7:6.

Daddy's Day of Judgment for the world is approaching. Please understand I am not predicting when Jesus is coming back. He wants us to be knowledgeable of what scripture says about who we are as a people and what the future holds for us. It was never taught to us what will happen to slaves and their descendants according to the bible.

Without the teachings of the apocryphal books, and other lost books that correlates with the bible; we are lost in who the bible identifies as the true Children of Israel.

These books give detailed information as to what happened, why it happened, and what will happen next concerning us and the world. Please read these apocryphal books last printed as part of the King James Bible in 1611. These books are still available with pictures of our ancestors that confirm who we are. We also need to read the book of Jasher, The I and II Book of Esdras, and the Book of Enoch to know what is happening to us and why. According to Isa. 60:2, darkness covers the earth, gross darkness covers the people meaning: there is no knowledge to us or the people of the earth as to who we truly are. I am a Mother to Israel sent to inform the Twelve Tribes of what is happening to us. This only applies to "True Israel".

Jacob's Trouble

In the book of Joel, it tells us the beginning of sorrows for the Children of Israel and eventual punishment of the world called 'Jacob's trouble', Jer. 30:7. We are now entering into the 'Valley of the dry bones' phase that was promised to Israel in Eze. 37. This is relevant to where we are today in the world. It is time for Israel's redemption from wherever we have been scattered among the heathen (nations) in the earth.

Joel 1:2-8, 13-15, 2 Here this, ye old men, and give ear, all ye inhabitants of the land. Hath this been in your days, or even in the days of your fathers? What God is asking is, has the whole family of Israel ever been exiled out of its land and sent into the world under a perpetual curse forever until the 400-year curse is complete? 3 Tell ye your children of it, and let your children tell their children, and their children another generation. 4 That which the palmerworm hath left hath the locust eaten; and that which the locust hath left hath the cankerworm eaten; and that which the canker hath left hath the caterpillar eaten. Before our ancestors were exiled, God sent these plagues on them up to the time they had to leave our land or fight unto death. 5 Awake, ye drunkards, and weep; and howl, all ye drinkers of wine, because of the new wine, for it is cut off from your mouth. 6 For a nation is come up upon my land, strong, and without number, whose teeth are the teeth of a lion, and he hath the cheek teeth of a great lion. This is when the Romans came and made war with our ancestors that lead to exile. 7 He hath laid my vine waste and barked my fig tree; he hath made it clean bare and cast it away; the branches thereof are made white.

8 Lament like a virgin girded with sackcloth for the husband of her youth. Now our covenant is broken with our father. He is a husband to Israel; for the land is our mother. We do not have an advocate in the earth to stand for us. We are alone and naked in the world without our father's protection. He was wroth with us because of our actions which he continually warned us against. We had to pay the penalty! 13 Gird yourselves and lament, ye priests: howl, ye ministers of the altar: come, lie all night in sackcloth, ye ministers of my God: for the meat offering and the drink offering is withholding from the house of your God. 14 Sanctify ye a fast, call a solemn assembly, gather the elders and all the inhabitants of the land into the house of the Lord your God, and cry unto the Lord. 15 Alas for the day! For the day of the Lord is at hand and as destruction from the Almighty shall it come.

Our punishment was set; it was time to leave the land of our inheritance. Joel 2:1, 12-13, 17-20, 23-27 1 Blow ye the trumpet in Zion, and sound the alarm in my holy mountain; let all the inhabitants of the land tremble: for the day of the Lord cometh, for it is nigh at hand; 12 Therefore, also now, saith the Lord, turn ye even to me with all your heart, and with fasting, and with weeping, and with mourning. 13 And rend your heart, and not your garments, and turn unto the Lord your God; for he is gracious and merciful, slow to anger, and of great kindness, and repenteth him of evil.

17 Let the priests, the minister of the Lord, weep between the porch and the altar, and let them say, spare thy people, O Lord, and give not thine heritage to reproach, that the heathen should rule over them: wherefore should they say among the people, where is their God? 18 Then will the Lord be jealous for his land and pity his people. 19 Yea, the Lord will answer and say unto his people, Behold, I will send you corn, and wine and oil, and ye shall be satisfied therewith: and I will no more make you a reproach among the heathen (nations). 20 But I will remove far off from you the Northern army. And will drive him into a land barren and desolate, with his face toward the east sea, and his stink shall come up, and his ill savor shall come up, because he hath done great things.

The priests and people had to come before God to weep and cry out for God to spare them while going through the punishment he assigned to us. God had the priests and people to make sacrifices and cry out for us, though they were crying out for themselves at the time they were gathered. Because the punishment had been set that we are presently living out. Israel, Jacob the end times is about us being eradicated from the earth and the remnant that God will not allow to be destroyed.

The descendants of his people must come home to be a people to him again. A note from the Potter and the clay Rom. 9:20-21. God is the potter and we are the clay. He made us for all different purposes. How can the clay tell the potter what purpose he will make him to serve? Just as Israel was warned by God that he is the potter and he choose what he wants to make for whatever purpose. He is the one who pluck up and pull down and to destroy it. He did this to his very own children. So, if he didn't spare us, how does the heathen think they can take territory and power to rule that belongs to our God? He will destroy the posers pretending to be Shem. Esau was firstborn, but God had another purpose for him. God is using Esau just as he used Pharaoh, to show his power of protection over Israel and that his name might be declared throughout all the earth, Rom. 9:17. We sinned and had to be punished.

God promised to restore us. We get a second chance, but the world will not get a second chance. Esau through Japheth committed identity fraud on us. They are posing as Jacob while the Ottoman Turks are posing as Shem. This is an abomination. A penalty will have to be paid because of these acts. They never believed that God would come back to redeem his people. They were under the assumption that our curse is perpetual without end. Rom. 9:12-13 says, the elder will serve the younger and Jacob have I loved, but Esau have I hated.

We are at the end of Gentile rule. At the blink of an eye the spiritual blinders on our eyes will be removed. The spiritual chains on our hands, feet and the yoke upon our shoulders will be destroyed. We will be free and will never suffer being exiled or spiritual death again. But before this happens Esau will try to exterminate us worldwide. A race war will be the order of the day. The Gentiles are seeing their kingdoms crumbling all over the world. Their foundation was built on sand. They trust in their father Satan, that defeated foe. They rule by wickedness and greed. Esau never had rule over Shem. We are the seed of Abraham, Isaac, and Jacob, people of the promise. Three gifts were given to us as our inheritance. They are kingship, priesthood, and royalty. Through our fall Satan was given opportunity to be God of this earth. He is ruling through Gentile rule. They think by taking the territories they conquered from us they can function and prosper without us. They don't accept us as God's people or God as their creator.

God says for these things they must die! 2 Esdras 8:1-3 Common English Bible (CEB) He answered me: "The Most High made this world for the sake of many but the future world for the sake of few. 2 But I will tell you a parable, Esdras. Just as when you ask the earth and it tells you that it provides much clay to make earthenware, but little dust from which gold comes to be, so the present world also works. 3 Many indeed are created, but few will be saved."

2 Esdras 9:1-22 Common English Bible (CEB) He answered me: "Measure carefully within yourself, and when you see that a certain part of the signs that were predicted have passed, 2 then you will understand that the time has come in which the Most High will begin to visit the world that he made. 3 When the movement of places, tumult of peoples, plotting of nations, inconstancy of leaders, and confusion of princes appear in the world, 4 then you will understand that it was about these things that the Most High spoke from former days, from the beginning. 5 Just as with everything that has happened in the world, the beginning is known from the end, [a] and the end

comes to be seen, 6 so also are the times of the Most High. The beginnings are manifest in prodigies and mighty works, and the end is evident in deeds and in signs. 7 All this who will be saved, who will be able to escape through their works or through the faith with which they believe 8 will survive the predicted dangers and will see my salvation in my land and within my borders, 14 which I have made holy for myself for a long time. 9 Then whoever has now abused my ways will be astonished, and whoever rejected them in contempt will linger in agony.

10 Those who didn't acknowledge me when they were alive, even though they received benefits; 11 those who despised my Law while they were enjoying freedom 12 and didn't come to their senses but continued to scoff while the opportunity for a changed life was still open to them—these people must acknowledge me in torment after death. 13 But don't be curious any longer about how the wicked will be tortured. Instead, inquire how and when the righteous, to whom the world belongs and because of whom the world exists, will be saved." 14 I answered, 15 "I said before and now will say again that those who perish are more numerous than those who are saved, 16 just as a wave is greater than a drop." 17 He answered me: "As the field is, so is the seed; and as the flowers, so also the colors; as the labor, so also the product;[b] and as the farmer, so the threshing floor. 18 There was a time in this world—when I was preparing for those who now are, before the world in which they would dwell was made for them—no one opposed me, because no one existed yet.

19 Now, however, those who have been created in this world—a world furnished with both an inexhaustible table and an endless pasture[c]—have become corrupt in their habits. 20 I considered the earth—and, observe, it was ruined. I considered my world, and, observe, it was in danger because of the intrigues of those who had come into it. 21 I saw and spared them with great difficulty; I saved for myself one grape out of a cluster and one plant out of a great forest. [d] 22 Therefore, let the multitude that was born without purpose perish, and let my grape and my plant be preserved, because I perfected these with much effort.

We are that grape and the church the one plant out of a great forest. Daddy God himself with his warrior angels will come to our defense. The President of the United States won the election with the support of the Alt Right. He promised them a new America without other nations of people in it but them. He gave them permission to make war on us. They see that they are losing a grip on their power structure.

America is broke. Trump promises to bring back jobs he cannot deliver. Since the NAFTA Trade, American companies have a cheaper way to produce goods and services without paying top dollar to their workers. Those companies will not bring jobs back because they will lose money. They have to pay American wages and not third world wages. Babylon is falling, and America is the daughter of Babylon, Ps. 137:8, and Zech. 2:7. We must separate ourselves from the daughter of Babylon. Rev. 18:4 says to come out of her so we will not be partakers of her sins and that we not receive her plagues.

We are strangers sojourning in a strange land. God is using Donald Trump to show his power and protection through and over his chosen people and that all men will know his name and wondrous works. He is showing Trump's heart which is black and void of love for others. He took the lowest of their wealthy men from among them to show the world their true identity and intentions to their shame. God made them feel secure enough to take their hoods off to expose their mindset and violent character. He is showing the world how Gentile rule is destroying the earth with power, greed, and money.

Daddy God is showing Donald Trump as 'Revealer in Chief, and his actions speak louder than words. Donald Trump is the perfect tool in God's hands because no man can control him; he is a self-willed man. He allows the police to abuse and kill us without repercussion because there is no advocate to stand for us. Donald Trump does not like us as a people. He showed it when he and his father discriminated against black people in their apartment buildings; they were sued. He promoted fallacies about the wrongful conviction of the Central Park 5 that happened in 1989. In 2002, a convicted rapist and murderer confessed to the crime. The Central Park 5 were exonerated because of DNA and paid a 41 million settlement. With all this evidence he still maintains his propaganda towards those 5 men. Donald Trump started the birther movement against our President Barak Obama. He and his cabinet members are trying to erase President Obama's legacy. President Obama your legacy will never be erased no matter what they do.

Daddy God gave you two terms nearing the end of Gentile rule. The presidency of Barak Obama signaled their end. The mess you inherited became better managed without a lot of bandages and tape. You had some real kingly ideals that you put in place. You were the most suave, President this country has ever had. You reigned with dignity and in excellence. You have swag that is the essence of gifted intelligence that comes from above. The presidency of Barak Obama is a foreshadow of things to come. It was ordained from the beginning to get people prepared for black Godly ruler-ship over the earth. Black ruler-ship was the order of the day up to the close of the 16th century.

The kingdom will be ruled by Jesus who happens to be of our ancestry and who looks like us because he is the first fruit from among us. We are an exceptional people with gifted intellect that causes us to excel in any field we choose to go into in the world. We have something the rest of the world don't have. We are shining lights. Jesus will send those whom he selected as kings/priests into the nations of the earth to represent the kingdom of God as his Emperors, Empresses, Kings, and Queens, and royalty. We are natural born rulers; we will govern with him in the kingdoms of the world. It is a part of our inheritance given to our forefathers Abraham, Isaac, and Jacob. We are the descendants, the children of God!

He is visiting the earth showing his great and mighty power. As soon as they rebuild, he sends more catastrophes to tear down. Esau always declares he will rebuild. But he didn't declare this over Puerto Rico, did he? They haven't yet begun to rebuild Puerto Rico and the storm happened in September 2017. America has limited resources; how will they keep rebuilding and survive as a nation too?

A race war has been declared on slave descendants in the United States. It is invisible but tangible. We were always told about this war and now 45, the President of the United States has sold us out to the Alt Right. They manifested themselves in Virginia by marching around with their tiki torches and chanting slogans. This is the start of tribulations and WWIII.

The difference between this war and all other wars is that Daddy God is coming to defend the remnant of his children that will be left. Donald Trump also signed a bill HR 1242 into legislation commemorating 400 years of African American achievements in America. Well, this same 400 years align with prophecy which speaks of exiled Hebrews being a stranger in a land that is not their own being mistreated, abused and enslaved for 400 years. But before Daddy God brings us out of our punishment, he will visit them who put us in bondage, then he will bring us out with great substance, Acts 7:6-7, which is our wealth that was taken when we fell and left a vacancy in the land of our inheritance. This is our present situation. Of all the Israelites that he scattered worldwide, only 12,000 per tribe will remain.

Israel/Jacob the end times is about us being eradicated from the earth and the remnant that God will not allow to be destroyed. The

Hebrew Year 5779 is the year of being birthed as a nation for Africans of the Diaspora and war with the dragon. Satan wishes to cut us off as a nation. The descendants of his children must come home to be a people to him again.

Who Am I?

He called me for such a time as this.

My name is Sharon Davis Green. My spiritual name is Em Sharon Yisrael, an Empress in Daddy's coming kingdom. I identify as a Hebrew bible believer whose homeland is Judea. I am of the Tribe of Judah. Jesus is my Lord and Savior. Like Deborah, I arose as a mother in Israel (Judges 5:7).

He has called me, an Empress, a mother to Israel, a messenger and a gatherer.

My spiritual training started when I was a small child around the age of 2 years old. My grandmother had us in church day/night and all day on Sundays. I always felt there was a river behind my grandmother's church, because spiritually as a little girl that's what I always envisioned when we were in service. No, there was not a physical river behind her church and I didn't know what significance it had at the time. 1 John 5:8 says the spirit, the water, and the blood are in agreement, that they bear witness in the earth. The spirit of God was definitely in my grandmother's church service and the blood is spiritually applied to our lives for protection. This all signified to me that God was telling me that I am spiritual and he gave me gifts in this area of my life for such a time as this.

I grew up in the racist south, Memphis, Tn. My grandmother frequently visited Cotton Plant and Brinkley, Arkansas; so, I witnessed the discrimination and hate. My parents tried to shelter us as much as they could against the evils of racism. As I grew, I would always tell people I was blessed. I would always see myself sitting in Jesus lap contented, surrounded by all the animals that were peaceful.

The first three of my mother's children were adopted within the family. My natural father's sister and her husband adopted my older sister and me. Another Aunt and her husband adopted my brother when we were ages 4, 3, 2. My natural father had a car accident that left him fighting for his life. He became paralyzed on one side with a metal plate on his brain. He had to learn to eat, walk, talk and function independently all over again. God blessed him to recover with disabilities.

My natural mother left Memphis and went to Chicago. She remarried and had six other children. She has nine children in total. My adopted parents were educators and professional people. My dad achieved his Doctorates degree in Education administering programs he designed for Memphis Board of Education. My mom's career started off as being a Social worker. She ended her career as a Professor teaching Psychology/Sociology at Memphis State University. I was raised very well to do. I left home to live in Chicago against my parents' wishes at seventeen years old to find myself. I needed to know my natural family in order to know who I was. They wanted me to go to college, but I was in rebellion.

Life went from sweet to bittersweet. My life became hard and the door shut behind me. I couldn't go back home. I was now along, afraid, and had to fend for myself against all odds. Things did not work out with my natural family like I had planned. There was no more guidance, mental, or financial support. I was on my own. I burnt bridges I never intended to burn.

I birthed three children into the earth which are sons.

I then got married in 1989, which resulted in a bad marriage. That's when my adult spiritual journey began. I had to learn to make God my God and not my grandmother's God or my parents God. My husband was physically and mentally abusive. I started to get in the Word (bible) to protect my children and myself. My marriage failed, I was now divorced after 9 years. God released me from that marriage in 1998 by using the spiritual warfare weapons I had learned; I stood on the Word until change came.

This is when God allowed me to see in the spirit realm and to experience it. He would get me up in the wee hours every morning between 3 or 4am to pray for our youth for about an hour daily for almost 5 years. I was a single parent again with young boys who were still in grade school. I lived in Holy City on the Westside of Chicago. Life was rough raising my sons alone.

In 1990 my biblical/spiritual training excelled by watching Pastor Creflo Dollar's television ministry. He had an on the edge of the seat type of teaching that excited and fed my spirit. He taught me how to operate in spiritual warfare. While sitting under Pastor Creflo, God gave me the first vision of my calling. He showed me myself as a woman dressed like Harriet Tubman running with a lot of children. We were all holding hands and running while bombs were going off behind us dropping from the sky like rain. They never got us, but it kept us running and snatching up children as we went. There were a lot of dead bodies lying all around on the ground, but we escaped! In this vision he was sending me out to gather the Children of Israel (which I didn't know at the time). My spiritual appetite began to increase, I wanted more.

It was 1991 when I was led to Crusaders West under Pastor Darryl O'Neal. Pastor O'Neal was another excellent teacher where I continued my spiritual growth for the next 11 years. In 1992 I started a business, Daramola Jewelry Designs making jewelry. I took classes to learn how to make fine jewelry working in 22kt gold and sterling silver using precious and semi-precious stones. I made beaded jewelry as well. I supplied high end boutiques with my handcrafted items and became a vendor to sale my jewelry at different events. In 1996 I landed a contract with Spiegel/E-Style catalog to produce 144 pairs of earrings. Spiegel/Essence magazine teamed up together to add an afro centric flair to their jewelry line. God gave me favor to receive $18 per pair for 144 pairs of earrings that was ordered from me. Their going rate was $15 per pair, I was elated! That contract was short lived, and I eventually got burnt out. I didn't understand why I didn't have continued success. I started losing faith of what God had told me.

God gave me another vision in 1998. I was on my way to an appointment I had that day. I had been in the spirit all that week and day. I didn't have a car at the time, so I used public transportation. I would put on my Walkman to sing, praise, and worship God freely while walking until I saw the bus coming. The bus would take me to the train line that runs along the expressway on Chicago's Westside. When I got to the Homan/Kedzie train platform, I heard an audible voice as I was praising and singing to God. Mine you, I had headphones on, I had to look around to see who was talking to me. Then the voice said, 'Are you ready?' I had to think on what did this mean? The voice asked again about three times, I answered and said, 'Yes Lord if you go with me every step of the way I'm ready'. Then he proceeded to say, "I'm taking you to higher heights, I'm giving you the things you asked for". He then turned my attention to the limousines on the expressway. Every time I looked up, I saw the most elegant limousines. He said to me, this is how you will travel. I was so amazed that I said, "Awwwh, this is what you are doing for me daddy." I was so elated I had a praise party with God that day! I came home and told my three sons that we are royalty and we were going to sit at the tables of Kings and Presidents.

My jewelry business wasn't doing what I wanted it to do so I went to school and reinvented myself. I worked a few jobs the next three years until I was blessed with a job driving city buses in 2003. For the next three years I didn't go to church much because of my erratic work schedule. I was thirsting to get back under the covering of a good Shepard again. The spirit directed me to Truth and Deliverance under Apostle John Abercrombie. Again, my biblical knowledge increased under him for about 6 years. While I worshipped under this ministry, God gave me a vision to make jewelry out of spiritual warfare weapons (Eph. 6:11-18) and the fruit of the spirit (Gal. 5:22-23). I drew them up and had them made in sterling silver. I decided to go with Men's cufflinks/tie pins and women's tag jewelry including a necklace, bracelet, and earring set. I tried to sell them but did not have great success at it. Now again I'm questioning God about is this what he wants me to do? How is some jewelry going to save souls? I gathered that it would bring money into the Kingdom for work to be done through the church, but I still didn't understand.

In 2006 God gave me yet another vision of my calling.

In this vision I saw a beautiful clean city with movable walkways. They flow throughout the city connecting it from one end to the other. There were a lot of people on the walkways standing as they were being transported to their destinations. They were dressed impeccably sharp! Everyone was on a specific business. I went into what looked like a plush hotel lobby. There was plush, luxurious, red velvety carpeting on the floor. The walls were made of exquisite red velvet with 24kt gold flowing thru it in intricate designs. There was a very tall but massive bank of elevator doors that was decked out in beautiful oak wood. The door opened, and other people were standing there with me waiting to get on. Everyone stepped aside, and I went on by myself. I pushed the top floor button. As I was in the elevator the floor of the elevator started rising up inside the higher, I got. The top of the elevator slid opened as I was rising up out of the elevator. I began to see the heavenly's.

I was high up in the atmosphere. I started to feel uncomfortable. There was an angel in a booth with wings flying around. He said, "come up here this is where you want to be". I had fear in my heart. But as I stepped out from the elevator the ground with each step became a transparent glass. With every step I took, a glass appeared. Then all the glass became one transparent sheet under my feet. God told me to look around. Everywhere I saw was infinity no matter which direction I turned to. God told me that as far as I could see I could have in any direction. Then God told me he was taking me to higher heights, that he was giving me the things I asked for. What he said brought to remembrance of him telling me the same thing on the train platform. So, I started to look in all directions and seeing an infinity without walls, borders, separations, or division. There was no ceiling cap. It just kept going, and going, and going. So, I claimed infinity in all directions! Then I politely apologized and asked if I could go back down to my comfort zone because this is too high for me. He allowed me to. I had this vision in my sleep. When I came back down in the elevator, I jumped straight up out of my sleep like I was there for real. It spiritually shook me. I started apologizing to the Lord and asking did I fail the test. Through the years, it would always bother me because I thought I missed it. That was the last vision God gave me. My season was up at Truth and Deliverance, it was time to move again.

I was led to Living Word under Pastor Bill Winston. I started attending Living Word around February 2009. Pastor Bill Winston is an amazing faith/prosperity teacher. My spiritual growth excelled under his teachings. I also had a friend; a sister in Christ named Linda Lucas. She was a member there and invited me to come to her church home. She was an entrepreneur and my travel partner. She became my jewelry rep and was working on getting my jewelry into Living Word Christian Center Bookstore. She and I went to President Barack Obama's Inauguration in January 2009. In March 2009 we went to Guadalajara, Mexico to find a jewelry manufacturer for my jewelry. Three weeks later we went to Shanghai, China in April of 2009 looking for manufacturers. A year later we lost Linda to cancer. I truly miss her.

I grew under Pastor Bill Winston but was thrown off track when I saw he included The Jewish flag into the pulpit. That flag didn't bother me until the Lord woke me up to my calling in June 2016. I brought it to Pastor Winston's attention, he said that flag belong to the Jewish people and they are the chosen people. Well, I couldn't accept his answer. That just didn't sit well with my spirit, so I had to leave in 2016.

In February 2012 Trayvon Martin was killed. I really got upset and couldn't stop crying and asking God why? Why is it this skin color we in get us killed? Why is it that people don't like our skin and hair? Why are we the scourge of the earth? What is it about this skin we are in? After continuing to ask and cry he finally answered me by taking me thru the bible, archeological artifacts, and historical events. Eventually he opened up my understanding. My research revealed pictures of who we were, where we came from, how we got here and why (Rom 10:3). It revealed who the people are posing as us. How it all tied into the end times. It revealed their plan to annihilate us and God's awesome plan to redeem his true people. All I thought I was going to do was reveal to black folks who they were. Look at what my research revealed; revelation knowledge Hallelujah!

God says wear your hair/skin as a badge of honor, it is a sign as to who you are. There is something incredible he has done to us. Like the bible says, he has sealed us to protect us from the world's "Day of Vengeance" that is coming to them, Rev. 7.

Now my calling is crystal clear. The whole puzzle of my life makes sense. I had to become an outcast in my own family to be able to identify with Israel as an outcast nation of people. I suffered what it means to be in poverty as a single parent mother, with and without a job. I never signed on for being a single-parent provider. This job requires two parents and/or a village for support. I understand our plight as a people under a curse. If I had stayed on the chosen path for my life; I would have gone to college, had a successful career, got married, had children, and lived in a big beautiful home. I would have done excellent for myself because of the background I came from. I had opportunity. Poverty and financial struggles were not a part of the life that I lived. If I lived a privileged lifestyle, I wouldn't have understood us as a people like so many of us who look down on each other do. We all believe that we have legitimate chance and opportunity to make life better for ourselves. I would have had that same judgmental attitude not realizing the playing field is unequal. They have double standards that don't include us, they only hinder us.

By being separated from my family, and enduring the adversities of my life, became training for such a time as this. To be his children, you must bear your cross and suffer for righteousness sake. We as a people have been enduring our sufferings for 398 years and counting. To get where Daddy God is taking us, we must suffer as strangers while being black, walking in the valley of the shadow of death until our exile ends.

During the first week of June 2016, Daddy God told me the curse of Deut. 28:15-68 has been broken over us and that he has redeemed us without money, Isa 52:3. He allowed me to hear a breaking noise in the spirit. He then said Eze. 37 are in effect. I realized that when the valley of the dry bones is resurrected; this is yet another phase of what we were not taught about the rapture. I'm so excited!!!!! Hallelujah! I never thought I would be left behind according to the teachings of the church. I cried because I didn't understand. But revelation knowledge revealed to me that I would stay behind to lead Israel back to our homeland; I was so exhilarated. I am much honored to be a chosen vessel for his purpose and will.

My assignment includes leading the remnant of twelve tribes of Israel to the Wilderness of Nations in our homeland. Because of the great race war that is coming to the world only 12,000 per tribe will be left, Rev 7:4. The end time is not about the end of the world per se. This is another lie of the enemy. It is about the end of Gentile rule over our lives and the world. Daddy God is coming back to claim legal rule over us, the earth, and his universe. This is happening in our lifetime!

Thank you, Daddy God, for using me as your vessel to achieve your purpose! My spirit rose up in me and became courageous and very bold; now I'm ready to go!

My name "Sharon" means a fertile plain that nourishes and promotes growth, Song of Solomon 2:1; this is one of Jesus characters, as The Rose of Sharon". A mother also nourishes and promotes growth in her children.

He has called me as an Empress to subdue nations. Like Deborah, Judges 5:13 says, "Then he made him that remaineth have dominion over the nobles among the people; the Lord made me to have dominion over the mighty. We will get all of our wealth and treasures back. "Daddy God has given me the task to go and claim ALL of our wealth and treasures back. It must be spoken into the atmosphere to reverse this spiritual curse in the presence of the leaders of the world. Everything that was taken from Shem must be returned. Shem includes all nations known in modern day time as the Middle East.

This is what Judges Chapters 4 and 5 says about who God has sent to lead Israel for such a time as this:

Deborah was a Judge/prophetess in Israel at the time King Jabin was King of Canaan. He oppressed the Northern tribes of Israel. Sisera was captain of Jabin's armies. Barak, an Israelite chieftain made war against the armies of Jabin. Deborah gives Barak a battle plan to follow. Barak tells Deborah if you go with me then I will go, but if you do not, I won't go. Deborah tells Barak she will surely go with him but lets him know that the journey will not be for his honor. God will sell Sisera into the hand of a woman, Jael. Deborah told Barak to get up and go take victory against Sisera, King Jabin and their armies. Has not the Lord gone out before you? Barak pursued Sisera and all his armies in hot pursuit. Sisera jumped out of his chariot and ran for his life. Barak continued to pursue the host of armies back to the Gentile city they came from with victory. Jael and her husband had a good relationship with Sisera, so he felt he could hide in her house and stay safe until he was able to escape. Jael was very nice to him. Sisera asked her for water, she gave him milk to drink. Sisera was very tired he needed rest; he was exhausted from the battle. Jael gave him cover to lie down and rest. She quietly went to him while he lay asleep and put a nail through his temple. He died. Barak came searching for him, Jael met Barak to show him where Sisera laid dead. God gave our ancestors victory on that day. They destroyed Jabin King of Canaan.

Then Barak and Deborah sang a song praising the Lord for avenging Israel when the people willingly offered themselves. They say awake, awake Deborah, awake and utter a song, a rise Barak and lead your captivity captive. Blessed above women shall Jael the wife of Heber the Kenite be; blessed shall she be above women in the tent. He asked for water and she gave him milk; she gave him butter in a lordly dish. She put her hand to the nail, and her right hand to the workman's hammer; and with it smote off his head, when she has pierced and stricken through his temples; at her feet he bowed, he fell, he lay down: at her feet he bowed, there he fell down dead.

"For the Lord hath created a new thing in the earth; a woman shall lead (teach) a man" (Jer. 31:22). God chose new leaders when war came to the city gates, but not a shield or spear was seen among forty thousand in Israel. My heart is with Israel's princes, with the willing volunteers among the people. I, like Deborah arose as a mother in Israel to lead the way. The Daughters of Zion are modern day Jael's who know the word, and who flows in the spirit of God. The princes of Israel are our men who are standing and fighting the destruction of our people. Those who flow in the word and spirit of God are the willing volunteers among our people who are not afraid. He has made us Warriors, the first line of defense in the earth. In Judges 5:8, it states there was not a shield or spear seen among forty thousand in Israel...this means that this war is spiritual as well as physical. God has given me the spirit of David, he has made me to sing, dance, and praise him.

We must fight spiritually. We have to move like Jesus did when he was in the earth. We slay the defeated demonic foe with the sword of the spirit that is in our mouth. The defeated demonic foes are those who are coming for our lives, the Alt Right and their associates. The 'Make America Great Again' people are this defeated demonic foe and those worldwide with Esau's mindset. Esau is still killing Jacob. Everyone will have to choose sides, there is no in between. Either you are for God, Jesus, and the true Children of Israel or you on Satan's team. There is no in between! "You will either love your fellow man with the love of God or you will hate with racism in your heart. How is your heart? This is all about your heart condition towards people.

We are in the same image as Jesus our Messiah. He has the Sword of the Spirit in his mouth and so do we. One can put one thousand to flight; two can put ten thousand to flight, imagine how many we can slay with more of us together! We are the righteous generation, Warriors for the great battle that will soon ensue! We are slayers of the defeated demonic foes. Satan and his kingdom have been conquered; when Jesus went into the grave and took the keys of the kingdom of sin and death and hung it on the cross to make a spectacle out of Satan, Rev 1:18. When he ascended up on high, he led captivity captive, and gave gifts unto men. So, Satan and his kingdom are literally under our feet. He does not have power over us anymore. We have authority over him and his demonic horde. We have the power to bind and loose, to declare a thing and watch it come to pass.

There is no advocate in the earth to stand for us as a people; we are twelve tribes. There is no one that will come to our defense. That is why we have been trained for this, sitting in those church pews on Sundays and in those bible classes. We defeat demonic foes daily in our everyday lives when Satan confronts us! For the just shall live by faith, we live by faith and not by sight! We flow in bringing forth natural things out of unseen things. For we believe, then we speak, when we speak, we see what we say utilizing our faith and the spoken word! That's who we are and that's how we roll! These are how our super powers materialize…it's in our faith and the spoken word y'all!

We are bold as lions and courageous unto death, because we know who got out backs! Daddy God is using us to lead the way into our jubilee. It's time for us to get busy and answer the call.

These are our marching orders. This is how Daddy God will deliver us from the hands of our captives/oppressors. A war cry will go out into the earth telling Israel wherever we are scattered to wake up to the spiritual awakening of Eze. 37. We are the valley of the dry bones. The Northern kingdom and Southern kingdom become one again. We will become a village as one people worldwide for our return home. There will be twelve thousand per tribe left from the great slaughter they will make on us worldwide. It's time to wake up Israel...our time has arrived to come into our inheritance as the descendants of the Children of Israel!

If he be for me, who could be against me....NO ONE! He says, "Do not be afraid of them, for the Lord your God himself shall fight for you Sharon and Israel, Deut. 22:3! There is no God besides him.... who can defeat him....NO ONE!!!! We are his namesake. He has gravened our name in the palm of his hand Israel. He is our re-reward!

Let's go Israel, let's go Jael's where you at!

This book is meant to be a study guide. It will take you on a journey to find ourselves as an exiled Hebrew people. Please have your bible, the apocryphal books, the Book of Jasher, and the book of Enoch which are

available online for enlightenment, to prove this information.

As you read please keep in mind that I'm speaking to all slave descendants and those Israelites scattered abroad to the four corners of the earth; we are The Children of Israel, a Hebrew people.

The Children of Israel went through the final exile from our homeland of Israel/Canaan at two separate times. The first Ten Tribes, Ephraim or Israel, were exiled around 721 B.C. and the Tribe of Judah and Benjamin were exiled between 70 C.E. to 134 C.E. We are the tribe of Judah that came in the last dispersion. For slave descendants to find ourselves, we must examine all factual data from the past that pertains to our ancient ancestral history. There were three major events that happened which lead us to our present condition in life. The first is Satan's fall from heaven that resulted in him becoming god of this natural world we live in. The second is Man's fall through Satan's deception. The third is our fall as God's children because we broke his commandments. Satan was given a certain time period to rule which coincides with our 400-year curse and punishment. He's ruling with wickedness through the Gentiles which also have 400 years to rule the earth. The curse is found under Deut. 28:15-68 and the 400 years is found in Gen. 15:13-14 and Acts 7:6 and the fall of Satan in Isa 14/Rev. 20.

It must be noted that where we came from; the land was inhabited by black people at that time (see pictures). When the first man Adam was created, it was from the clay of the earth which was the same skin color of black people. We were created in God's image. He is black like our skin color. A vicious lie was told to promote propaganda that God, Jesus, and the biblical characters of the bible is Caucasian. It is stated in 1 Maccabees 3:48 they painted the likes of their images in the Book of the Law. This is how they all became white in the bible pictures. As a part of our punishment, all knowledge that identifies who we are, was covered up; hidden. We died spiritually which put us in a stupor of not knowing who we are. All of our spiritual knowledge was taken away, so we would not figure a way out of our punishment, Isa 3:1-3. The adversary went to great means to hide us in plain sight. We were stripped of our identity and our ancient heritage. In my research, I have found the "powers that be" that stole us knows our identity. They will also tell us that the people of the black lands are not us even though they look like us and have the same skin complexions and hair.

The oppressors stole our ancient historical identity and claimed it as their own. They stripped us and confused knowledge. This became a rabbit hole filled with lies and deceit. The deeper we dig the more we find inconsistencies in their so-called ancient his-tory. It was all stolen and some of it made up. The nations of Israel, Syria, Iraq, Iran, Saudi Arabia, and Anatolia, Turkey are all Shem and are all black people. Esau/Japheth stole all of Shem's lands, wealth, and treasures. Daddy God wants it back. He gave it to us as our inheritance. These were known as "The Black Lands" the continent of Africa whose name was Alkebu-lan. They scattered us and then parted God's land and split the "Middle East" from the rest of Africa, Joel 3:2.

We are slave descendants exiled from our homeland of Israel, in the Middle East. The apocryphal books give us this information. We come from the North Central part of Alkebu-lan (Africa) in the land of Canaan which became Israel. We are all a black people; Hebrews who came from Shem. This is our ancient ancestral past.

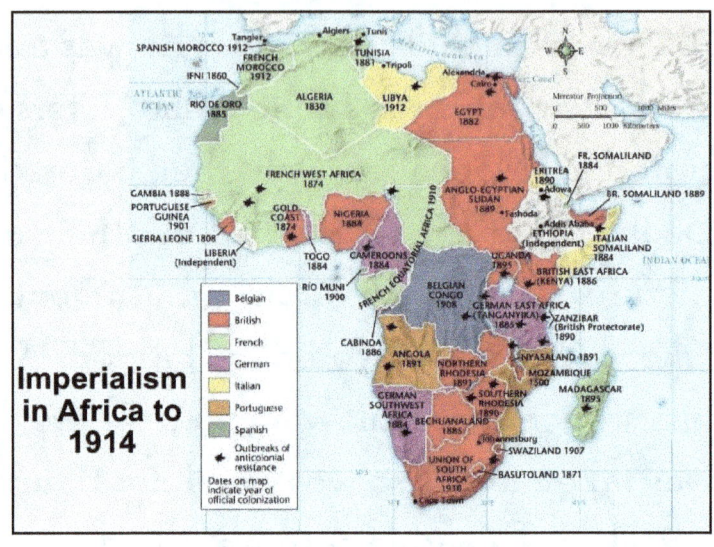

The "powers that be" never wanted us to find out who we are as a people because Gentile rule is the end of this age. Great lengths were taken to hide and destroy our history. All notable ancient civilizations all over the world were black. These were the Northern Ten Tribes, Ephraim. I have included their pictures in this book along with bible scriptures and actual historical dated events that all corroborate each other's existence. The Oppressors buried the truth, but now it is revealed. It is said the black man has no contribution to society. Read the proof I present; that will shake up your understanding and make you question everything you thought you knew and were taught. Then do your research to prove what I say is true.

We carry a spiritual darkness that causes us to be confused and suffer from identity crisis. At some point Hebrews were forced to choose foreign religions in exchange for freedom. We began following the Gregorian or Roman calendar and observing their day of rest which is Sunday. The day that was set aside for rest to worship on Sundays was reserved for their god, Apollo or Jupiter which is Satan, instead of observing the Sabbath day on Saturdays according to the Hebrew calendar.

It was always intended that we remained permanent slaves according to the slave laws. The oppressors reasoning was that God ordained our captivity and a perpetual curse to accompany it. With that being so, we were constantly warned by God through the prophets of the punishment and curses we would have to suffer. We were going to be punished for breaking our end of the covenant Yahweh made with our forefathers. Our oppressors thought that Daddy God abandoned us forever and gave us to them to do to us what they pleased. They think that our end is in their hands. I beg to differ regarding the scriptures of his holy word, and the apocryphal books.

It has been taught not to read the Old Testament because it does not apply to Christians today. This is in part true. The Old Testament is about the Children of Israel but also is a reference to where the world is going. However, it does apply to slave descendants, who are the Hebrew people. The Apocrypha Books, the Book of Jasher, and The Book of Enoch are other books that need to be read. They give the full story which the King James Bible only touches on. These books open up understanding concerning Old Testament bible stories. They give additional accounts of bible stories which clarifies what happened and why. They tell us what will happen to us in the end times. This is the why the Christian church need to read these books, so they will know what will happen as well.

This punishment of being exiled caused us to lose power, wealth, and control over our ancient land, wealth, kingship, priesthood, royalty, language and history, Dan 12:7b. We were stripped! Power/wealth transferred, and" The first became last." Only God's people were to suffer the punishment and curse of Deut. 28:15-68 which were to last 400 years and the afflictions of slavery according to Gen.15:13-14 and Acts 7:6.

Let's delve in deeper to find out how all of this started, where we are now and where we are going next to make an indelible mark on history changing times and power structures. The coming Kingdom will be in this order of the Kings/Priests picture figure A. This is the order of Daddy God's heavenly government on earth through the Children of Israel, Matt.6:10. It was set up in the form of the United Kingdoms of Great Britain and Europe…it's our time…it's our turn. "In the order of this picture, we rise as a new Godly Nation; as the Kingdom of Righteousness.

"Holy Icon of All the Saints of The Isle"

Who Are We?

We are a people who are going through the punishment/curse of being exiled from our homeland of Judea in Israel/Canaan. The punishment of Deuteronomy 28:15-68 included slavery and the curse of being black in America. The Gentiles look at us as a nation of people who are cursed and counted for nothing. They think this is our end forever, cursed without redemption or restoration. They think that we forfeited our inheritance, with no way of obtaining it. The world believes that we are the scourge of the earth, and our status as being cursed forever.

Where in his word does it say we are cut off forever? There is no scripture found anywhere that agrees with their thought process, no, not NONE! But the Gentiles will have you to think that the "Replacement Theory" is true. As if the church has replaced the Israelites, ha! Don't make me laugh at such ignorance, Rom 11:2, 5, 11-21. No one can replace us! The world is looking at those greedy Khazars who don't accept Jesus and call themselves Jews, perpetrating the true 'Children of Israel". They have convinced the world that they are us.

The true Children of Israel have an inferiority complex about us. It results from being brainwashed for 246 years. We were and are treated as three fifths humans, second-class citizens who are worthless and expendable. Our past was erased, carefully planned to disconnect us from our identity. We were such a blessed, protected, and powerful people, that Esau and Satan went to great lengths to hide us in plain sight, Psalms 83:3-8! Our oppressors are afraid of us finding out who we are because it signals their end, 2 Esdras 6:9. They are the end of things whereas, we are the beginning...the first shall be last, and the last first, Matt. 20:16. The world is out of sync. The operation of the world will switch back to the natural order of things at the end of Gentile rule. Satan has authority to be God over the earth during his fall. His authority extends to the completion of his time to be in rebellion against God. He fell from on high as an archangel.

He was the Bright Morning Star, very beautiful to look upon. He was the Archangel over Praise and worship; which is why imaging and music is so powerful today. Satan fell because he rebelled against and exalted himself over God. He imagined himself to be more powerful than God and lost his place in God's Heavenly Kingdom. He was kicked down to earth where he rules in wickedness in heavenly places and on earth, Isa. 14:12/Rev. 12:7-12. He has also carved out a special people for himself. It is Esau and the "Huns" which are "serpent people". The Huns separated into two groups of people. They are the Khazars who assumed our identity and the Ottoman Turks who assumed the original Arabs and Middle East identity. These "serpent people" are barbaric in nature. I go into detail about them later in the Chapter on Esau. Satan was given a time period to rule, until the fullness of the Gentiles comes in, Luke 21:24 or let's say 400 years which coincides with the

completion of our punishment. Esau via Satan's power and ruler ship did not start at the beginning of time, but rather as a result of Satan's fall. The power of Satan and his kingdom is under our feet. Jesus stripped Satan of the power of death and the sting of the grave. When his children and believers die, they only go to sleep to awaken to life, not death. But the unbelievers die unto death. They will awaken to the second judgment called the "Great White Throne Judgment".

Our oppressors are identified as Esau (through Satan), who is the twin brother to our progenitor Jacob and the "serpent people", The Ottoman Turks and the Khazars/The Huns/Japhet.

Esau still wants the position of the first born and birth rite as "Inheritor". But this Inheritance didn't come by the natural way of things, Yahweh Sabaoth designed it. He chose Jacob who he renamed Israel. He said, "Jacob I love but Esau I hate", Malachi 1:2-3.

Indigenous Indians

The ten Northern tribes were exiled around 721 b.c. They were taken captive by the Assyrians but broke away from them into freedom. Other people were brought in to replace them in their original homeland. Being exiled, they became the indigenous Indians of the land throughout the world. They came to America and settled here before it was named America.

The twelve tribes are all in captivity and have experienced slavery via the transatlantic slavery or being indigenous to this country before colonialism and colonization. How is that possible? Gen 10:25, during the time of Peleg that the earth was divided. This lines up with the time of the Tower of Babel. Men went everywhere in the earth before the land mass divided.

We are Judah in North America. Benjamin is in South Africa. The Ten Northern tribes scattered everywhere to the four corners of the earth. They became the Olmec Indians. They were the black Mexicans, the Aztecs, and the Mayans, and Indians of the Americas. They were the indigenous people of the land before Japheth in Gen: 10:5 inhabited their lands. They set up their kingdoms and flourished until our eventual downfall. A time for Satan to rule through Gentile rule. It affected all black civilizations where we lost our power and authority. We are all prisoners of war under the Jus Gentium to Rome until the times of the Gentiles are fulfilled, Luke 21:24.

There is not much information about the black Indians after 1492. They have been hidden from history.

Time started counting towards the fulfillment of the curses of Deuteronomy 28 and the fulfillment of Gentile rule, Luke 21:24 when slavery started in 1619. Power and wealth transferred where we became dispossessed and wiped out of history.

What mystifies my mind is, how did they think they could get away with erasing us out of history, hiding us in plain sight, and we not find out about it? Didn't they know our daddy was coming back for his children, Isa 41:8-9? He promised to wake us up from our slumber, to resurrect us Eze. 37. Don't they know that he won't substitute his children for anyone else? He said he created us for himself and we shall show his praise, Isa 43:21. That is why we are singers, dancers, poets, musicians, and the like. We show our praise through these, and much other intellectual giftedness. So how is it that Esau and the nations think that they can continue to terrorize us, kill us, disenfranchise us, and afflict us without repercussion from our heavenly father? It is an understatement to say what they do to us now, determines the greater degree of them reaping what they are sowing. We are their blessing under Gentile rule for a certain period of time!

God allowed his people who are stiff necked and hard hearted to be punished in the hands of Esau and the oppressors among the nations. They terribly mistreated God's children. We personally have not done anything to none of these people, Isa 52:5. These Gentiles hated us without a cause. The Oppressors got in the way of family business. This was a punishment and curse we had to endure. We are suffering because we didn't have daddy's protection and we had to leave our land. The heathen Esau is allowed to do what he wants to do to us without repercussion, for a certain period of time. They should have read where he said, "Those who bless us are blessed, but those who curse us are cursed, Gen. 12:3. They should have paid attention in their zeal and lust for our blood. Seems to me they kill us as sacrifices to their God Apollo/Jupiter/(Satan). Remember, God said Jacob I love, but Esau I hate. Esau is the heathen and he is barbaric. Look at how he's treated us and the world up to this point.

Our father says we are gravened upon the palms of his hands, he cannot forget us. He says a mother may forget her child she is nursing but he will never forget us, Isa 49:15-16. Power and wealth will transfer back into our hands as it was before. He made us a nation of Kings/Priests, Rev. 5:10. We were the original lawgivers that failed, Psl 60:7. We are still paying our debt for the sins of our fathers and their mindset against God which many of us carry that very same mindset today.

With this new knowledge, we all should start to treat each other better because we are connected. We are a holy and royal people. Yahweh says he will call us out of all the places he sent us among the heathen for his namesake, because his name is on us, Isa. 48:11. Our father has promised to restore us. He will give us a pure language to call upon the Lord with one voice.

Figure 1Zharsky, Natalia "Archangel Michael"

Civilization started in Africa, originally called Alkebu-lan "The Black Lands". Ancient archaeological finds show the black people that built and inhabited the Kingdoms of Syria (The Assyrians), Iraq (Babylonians, Chaldeans), Iran (Persians), Arabia (Black Arabs), Egypt (Egyptians), Turkey (Anatolians) and Israel (Hebrew Children of Israel). All of these nations are scattered as well. They were not all wiped out. We all lost control of our kingdoms. Power, wealth, and control of our lands transferred to Gentile ruler ship via Satan.

This is our story Slave descendants, Hebrew people, Israelites in the Americas and worldwide wherever we have been scattered as an exiled people. We are a peculiar people. There are none other people on the planet like us. We are people of the light. As I stated before, we are spiritually dead. Let's remember we are spirit beings, having a natural experience, in these flesh bodies that provides us with our earth-suits, as long as we are alive in the earth. We are spirit beings first. As God's children we have a direct spiritual connection to him. I go into detail in the chapter on "The Pineal Gland." There are so many scriptures in the old and New Testament about God's light and the glory of God. Let's see why this is important to us as a people.

Isa. 60:1-2 says, "A rise and shine for the glory of the Lord has risen upon you." That glory that shall rise upon you is how he will separate us. The glory will illuminate us like this picture. *"Scene from "Voroneţ Monastery"*

We have always been warned about a race war. He says, "Do not be afraid of them, for the Lord your God himself, will fight for you," Deut. 3:22. We will need to be bold and brave because we will arise. Like the Phoenix rising from the ashes yall, that's us. Except we are royalty, we are the real thing, not a mythical thing like the Phoenix! It is time for us to get in our proper places. Sons of God and Daughters of Zion, we are about to be revealed according to Isa. 60:1-2.

It is ironic that we have been the secret this whole time, The Hidden Ones, The Children of Israel. We are the kingdom people that will light up the world. I know that will be a beautiful sight to behold. We will escape the coming judgments meant for the world. We have already been tried in the fire Please understand that we are completing a 400-year curse/punishment. The world's punishment is not meant for us. This is why he says come out of her, Rev. 18:4. It's time for God's retribution on the world because of the way they dealt with us in our 400 years of punishment, and because they turned their backs on God.

Isa. 60:1-2 says, "Arise and shine for the glory of the Lord has risen upon you." That glory that shall rise upon you is how he will separate us from those who are posing as us. The glory will illuminate us just as it did Moses when he went up to the mountaintop to get the Ten Commandments, Ex. 34:29-30. We are kingdom people, the first family of the earth. We are the Elite! We will hold these titles again just as we held them in Great Britain/Europe before Gentile rule took affect:

Duke (male) or duchess (female) is a member of the nobility, historically of highest rank below the monarch, and historically controlling a duchy.

Marquess or marquis is a nobleman of hereditary rank. In the British Isles the title ranks below a Duke and above an Earl.

Earl is a member of the nobility. The title is Anglo-Saxon, akin to the Scandinavian form jarl, and meant "chieftain", particularly a chieftain set to rule a territory in a king's stead. In Scandinavia, it became obsolete in the Middle Ages and was replaced with duke. In later medieval Britain, it became the equivalent of the continental count (in England in the earlier period, it was more akin to duke; in Scotland it assimilated the concept of mormaer).

Count (male) or countess (female) is an aristocratic nobleman in European countries. The British equivalent is an Earl (whose wife is a "countess", for lack of an Anglo-Saxon term).

Chancellor is the title of various official positions in the governments of many nations.

Baron is a title of nobility. The word baron comes from Old French baron, itself from Old High German and Latin (liber) baro meaning "(free) man, (free) warrior"; it merged with cognate Old English beorn meaning "nobleman". The mediaeval Latin word baro, baronis, was used originally to denote a tenant-in-chief of the early Norman kings, which class developed into feudal barons who held their lands from the king by the feudal tenure per baroniam and were entitled to attend parliament.

Lord is a deferential appellation, in the majority of cases non-official, meaning in general "one with power and authority, a master or ruler". The king is frequently referred to in mediaeval documents as "The Lord King". The official peerage titles of Baron, Viscount and Earl may be replaced with the unofficial generic appellation of "Lord", either in written or spoken use.

Sir: as a knight, this was a member of a class of lower nobility in the High Middle Ages.

All creation is waiting for the 'Sons of God' to be revealed, Rom. 8:19. When this happens, even the land has to spring into action to be able to support us at our return to the homeland of our inheritance, Eze.36:8. I will start at the beginning so we can trace ourselves into this present day and time. But we will bounce around at times to make connections to give us a complete picture of what was, is, and still to come.

The Flood

In the book of Genesis, the ninth chapter, we read about Noah and his three sons Shem, Ham, and Japheth. Through their seed, they replenished the earth. The Lord caused a great flood to cleanse the earth of non-belief in him and the worship of idol gods, violence, and bloodshed. It lasted 40 day and 40 nights. While on their voyage, Ham committed a sin against his father. Ham saw his father's nakedness Gen. 9:22. What this means is that Ham made light of his father's nakedness in his drunken state and told his brothers. This was an evil act. Ham was found righteous when Noah and his family were saved from the flood. By Canaan being one of Ham's offspring, Noah cursed his son instead before he was born. The father's punishment fell on the son.

Noah cursed Canaan to be slaves of slaves or servants of servants in Gen. 9:25. When power transfers back to our ruler ship, Canaan will become our slaves; note slave of slaves. In Gen 9:27, God shall enlarge Japheth, and he shall dwell in the tents of Shem; and Canaan shall be his slave or servant. What this means is, Japheth is living in the tents of Shem by pretending to be Shem. Shem is the original people of Israel, Syria, Iraq, Iran, Saudi Arabia, and Anatolia, Turkey. The modern day people who are claiming these nations are posing as Shem. They are the Khazars and Ottoman Turks. They are imposters according to Gen. 9:27. They are living in the tents of Shem. By Canaan being cursed, the oppressors made us to fit this narrative. They chose a very clever way to operate in identity theft. Notice, identity theft is the leading crime of today! This is because it was done to us first as the nations of Shem. This is reciprocity of reaping what they have sown…now everyone is under attack!

To identify which one of Noah's sons that slave descendants came from, we must go to the maps in the back of your bibles. The map called "The Table of Nations" shows what land Shem, Ham, and Japheth's descendants peopled. The way you know you are Shem, is because Abraham, Isaac, and Jacob are from Shem. They are our

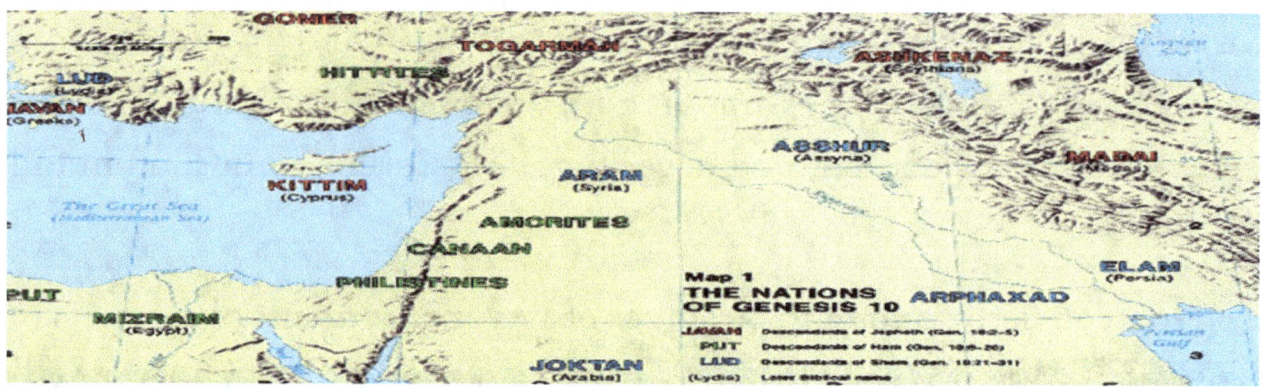

ancestors. They were not called Gentiles like we are called today in order to keep us confused and lost.

Psalms 83 tells us what the nations around us, did to us that cause us to cease from being a nation. We are the only people on the face of the earth that don't know our ancestral past, or who we are as a people. Every nation of people can identify who they are and where they come from.

As we see who we are today under the lineage of Shem, we can trace it all the way to Father Abraham in Gen.15:13-14/ Isa. 54:3-8.

This is where our forefather and his seed were chosen out of all the people of the earth to be a family to God. Yahweh made us his people and he became our personal father, kinsman redeemer, and family protector! We are personally our heavenly Father's children, connected directly to him and him to us. That makes my soul leap for joy and my spirit excited with anticipation, of being reunited with our Father/Jesus in our homeland he is calling us back to.

There are some major players that you need to learn about and keep up with as we chart out our history. They are Esau who is Edom (Rome), twin brother to Jacob; Ishmael the Arab nation who is Abraham's eldest son by Hagar the slave woman, and Japheth, whose seeds are The Khazars and Ottoman Turks. They are the same people under the name of The Huns which are identified by other names among the nations.

Yahweh told our forefather Abraham to leave his father's land and go to a place he was taking him to that flowed with milk and honey. It's where he promised to give an inheritance of land to father Abraham and his descendants forever. Father Abraham believed and went where God had led him. Abraham fathered two sons, Ishmael and Isaac. Ishmael was born of the slave woman, but Isaac was born of the free woman.

Two Covenants

We have two covenants here Gal. 4:21-31. Hagar represents the covenant of Mount Sinai whose children are born into slavery. Even though Mt. Sinai is a mountain in Arabia, it represents Jerusalem in its present state; for she is in slavery with her children, meaning we became like Hagar/Ishmael; we are under the curse and punishment of slavery, bondage, and afflictions. Hagar is still in the house. Sarah kicked her and her son out, so Isaac wouldn't be subjected to his brother. But because we are stiff-necked and hard-hearted, we are representing Hagar. When our punishment is over, we will be free like our true mother Sarah, who represents The New Jerusalem. But for the remainder of our punishment, we are exiled while our motherland suffers from Gentiles living on her as if they are her children. She is in distress just like we are. Isaac represents the promise of the New Jerusalem whose children are born free by the spirit of God through Jesus. This scripture is showing how Abraham's children of the promise through Isaac were slaves like the eldest son Ishmael and his mother. The promise was given to Isaac not Ishmael. Ishmael and Hagar are sent away because they cannot share in the promise of the freeborn son Isaac. We have the promise of Gen. 15:13-14/Acts 7:6-7, which will bring us out of our present-day system of bondage and exile, where we have been scattered. We are redeemed from the punishment of the curse of Deut. 28! We are redeemed Israel!

Isaac

Two sons, a set of twins were born to Isaac. Their names were Esau and Jacob. Esau was the older twin as he was born first. The promise fell on Jacob instead of Esau. By code, the first born always get the inheritance, but not by God's standards, the elder will serve the

Figure SEQ Figure * ARABIC 2 Gerome, Jean-Léon "Moses on Mount Sinai" 1895-1900

younger Gen. 25:23. Now watch this because it gets tricky. Esau is the older twin brother who sold his birthright for food, all on the account he was famished. Rom. 9:13 tells us, "As it is written, Jacob have I loved, but Esau have I hated". Gen. 27:6-30-45 tells us that Jacob and his mother schemed on Esau to obtain his spiritual blessing by fraud. The very same blessing Yahweh promised Abraham was passed down to Isaac and now to Jacob instead of Esau. Esau is livid because Jacob supplanted his brother twice in one day. He took the first-born blessing of birth rite and then stole the spiritual blessing which Yahweh intended for Jacob all along Rom. 9:10-13. Esau vowed to kill Jacob. In the present-day age, we are living in, Esau is still trying to exterminate Jacob to remain in power/wealth of the world. Esau became one with Rome. Today Rome is the modern-day Vatican, The Catholic Church and all their tentacles.

This is a key to understanding what is really going on with us, descendants of the children of Israel and our Caucasian oppressors, Esau/Rome, Ham, and Japheth.

The Place Pineal

In Gen 28: 11- 19/ Gen. 32:24-25, 29, 31 Jacob wrestles with someone. The identity of that someone is God. It wasn't meant to be a physical wrestling match but a spiritual one. God took Jacob to a place inside himself in the center of the brain, where we have a pineal gland. This special gland connects us to our heavenly Father for a one on one connection. Jacob saw the angels ascending and descending a ladder that reached up to heaven with the Lord standing above it. The Lord told Jacob that it was he, the God of Abraham and Isaac his fathers and told him of the promises he was giving to him and his seed. What Jacob actually saw was the spinal column in our body and that Holy place called pineal in the center of the brain. It is a direct two-way communication that connects us to the face of God and him to us. The melanin in our skin absorbs light which is stored as vitamin D. At the proper time, it will cause us to radiate like the sun. This is why the sun will no longer be needed because we will replace it.

We are a third eye people. We once had spiritual sight. It was cut off and we became spiritually dead without sight. At the designated time it awakens with new life. We will be able to see spiritually again. Our third eye or Pineal gland is how God communes with us and work through us. We are one with him. It is our super on our natural along with the Word of God. It is our spiritual warfare weapon.

This is how the remnant will make it through.

The promise of Gen. 28:14-15 says, "And thy seed (descendants) shall be as the dust of the earth, and thou shalt spread abroad to the west, and to the east, and to the north, and to the south: and in thee and in thy seed shall all the families of the earth be blessed. And behold I am with thee and will protect thee in all places whither thou goest and will bring thee again into this land for I will not leave thee, until I have done that which I have spoken to thee of.

In present day time we have been exiled into all the nations of the earth. We were the blessing to the nations of the world; but they terrorized and kill their blessing all day long. God is protecting Israel/Jacob until we return to our homeland. Yahweh Sabaoth is his name the Holy One of Israel is your redeemer, he is called God of the whole earth, and he is husband to our motherland Israel, Isa 54:1-10. He is our Heavenly Father. He promises to bring her children back home to her and make her the splendor of the world again. We have an awesome date with destiny!

As we run after Yahweh with all of our hearts, we begin to worship and serve him in spirit and truth. When we receive Jesus as our Lord/Savior it becomes a lifestyle and the Kingdom of God is realized within us. He imprints on us as we experience personal relations with him in prayer, praise, and spending time in his presence; pure and divine. That's love!

We can now conceptually visualize our complex spiritual connection to our father. He literally created us in his image, as people of the light. The pineal gland acts as a light cell in our brains. We are the only nation of people sealed in our foreheads with the ability to light up like him.

We are now in the time frame of being spiritually awakened according to Eze 37 the "valley of the dry bones." Spiritual life is starting to flow again; our spiritual eye or pineal gland is being awakened for our special time of being revealed according to, Rom. 8:19. The deeper our relationship, the more power and gifts we receive. We have gifts inside of us that need to be stirred up.

We are supposed to operate in the earth like Jesus did when he was here. He said 'GREATER' works than these (the works he did) will we do also, John 14:12. At the designated time, our spiritual eye will emit light that will cause our faces to illuminate like Moses did when he was in the presence of God. We are 'people of the light, kingdom people.'...we light up yall!

Egypt

The Children of Israel ended up in Egypt because of great famine in the land. Joseph was younger than his brothers with the exception of Benjamin the youngest of them all. Joseph was loved by his father who gave him a coat of many colors. His brothers hated him because they knew their father loved him more than the others. Joseph was also braggadocious about a dream he had, where his parents and brothers would bow down to him. His brothers got rid of him by putting him in a well and sold him to a group of Midianites who were on their way to Egypt. Joseph became Governor, second in command to Pharaoh in the kingdom of Egypt. His vision fulfilled itself and his brothers did bow down to him. Joseph's life was altered, so God could use him to have position and authority in Egypt, to preserve the lives of the Hebrews from famine.

The Hebrews outgrew the Egyptians. They complained to the new Pharaoh, who did not have the same relation with Joseph. The Hebrews found themselves in slavery which lasted 430 years. At the end of their captivity, they stripped the Egyptians and set out for the promise land Yahweh was giving them. Because of our disobedience and Egypt (bondage) mindsets, our ancestors had to wander around in the wilderness forty years to root out unbelief and fear. The older generation could not inherit the promise land because they didn't trust, believe, or obey Yahweh. They had to die off. The journey should have taken only 11 days according to Deut. 1:2.

Important point to remember about the wilderness experience in Ex.32:34-35 is when the children and Aaron made the golden calf, Yahweh said on that day of visitation, he would punish our ancestors; where we would be exiled from our homeland and sent into slavery and afflicted 400 years according to Gen. 15:13-14/Acts: 7-6-7. While the Children of Israel were in the land of their inheritance given to them by God, they broke his covenant. Our Ancestors were warned in Deut. 28 of the blessings or curses to choose for ourselves; either to obey our father Yahweh or worship idol gods like the heathen nations around us were doing. We eventually chose the curse. Yahweh left nations in the land that Joshua did not drive out to oppress us and take us into captivity as part of our punishment. Psalms 83 tells us how Esau and the nations around us got

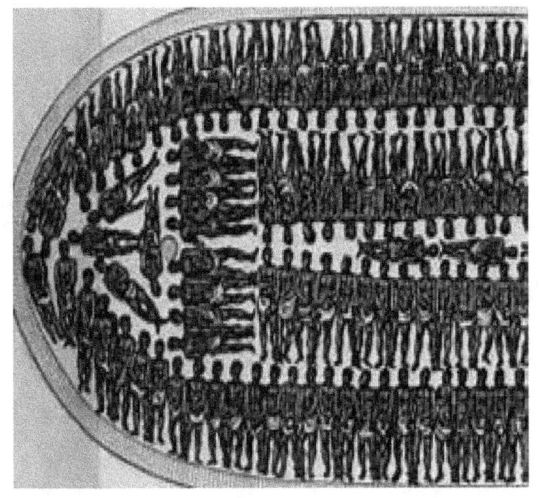

together to erase the association of our name Israel/Judah with the identity of slave descendants, out of the earth. We were hidden in plain sight with our identity and ancient culture stolen. They enslaved some of our ancestors and killed the rest who did not escape, fulfilling the curse of Deut. 28:15-68. The irony of the situation is, they have been masquerading around us all this time pretending to be us and claiming our history.

This is another key to understand why we don't have a heritage, culture, a language, or any form of identity other than Africans. The Africans (Ham) will tell you that we are not native to their lands. The reason the world accepts these rogue nations as if they are us is, they agreed to allow the lie to persist in stealing our identity. They started claiming our identity as early as 740 ad. By the 13th century they became us by assuming our name, power/wealth. They are the Gentiles who are destroying the world through wickedness, power, and greed. This is because they are Esau and Satan are their rulers and God. He is God of this world, 2 Cor. 4:4. They were not given the perpetual gift of ruler ship. Kingship, Priesthood, and Royalty is our inheritance, given to us by God for eternity!

Northern Kingdom vs. Southern Kingdom

Isa. 9:21 tells us that Manasseh, Ephraim (Northern Kingdom); together shall be against Judah (Southern Kingdom). For all this his anger is not turned away, but his hand is stretched out still. This is why we have black on black crime. These two kingdoms are still at war with each other today. Isa 3:2-5, 12 tells us God put the youth over us in the form of gangs. He took our men of authority away and all of those who could help us figure a way out of our punishment of the curse of 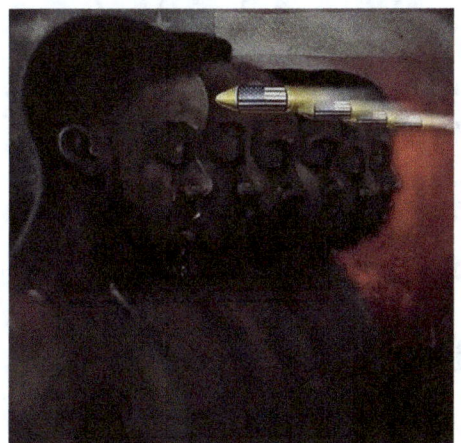 Deut. 28. We were cursed with being single parent mothers raising our male children alone.

Children are the black community's oppressors. They behave themselves proudly against the older people, there is no respect. They feed the prison system which has become a modern-day slavery system and big business. This is the reality of the black community today. He did this because he knew if we had any freedom from our present-day distresses, we would forget him and turn our backs on him. So, he allowed them to affect us all, rich and poor to keep us on our knees seeking him. He did it to turn our hearts to him through our troubles for his protection. He says we are a stiff-neck people.

Northern Kingdom vs. Southern Kingdom (cont.)
(1Kings 12:20-33)

A political schism took place where the kingship shifted from the House of David-Rehoboam, to Jeroboam of the Northern Kingdom. Rehoboam was going to fight to take the kingdom back, but God said no! What was being done is of Yahweh's doing. Rehoboam and his men went back home.

The religious schism happened when Jeroboam committed a greater evil than any of his predecessors by making idol gods of cast metal and provoking God to anger. Jeroboam and the Hebrews turned their backs on Yahweh, 1 Kings 14:9. 1 Kings 14:14-16, Yahweh says he will set a king over Israel who will put an end to the House of Jeroboam. The Northern Kingdom Ephraim was exiled in 721 B.C.

This also happened in 1 Maccabees 1:1-9, 20-24, 41-50 (The Apocrypha), where a Roman King ruled over Israel and Jerusalem whose name was Antiochus Epiphanes. In the time of Judah's exile. He was one of Alexander's officers that became kings over their own regions after Alexander's death. When Antiochus was king over the Greeks in the 107th year of the kingdom of the Greeks trouble emerged from Israel. A set of renegades led many people astray; this is the passage of scripture:

1 Maccabees 1:11 (b) "Come," they said, "let us ally ourselves with the Gentiles surrounding us, for since we separated ourselves from them many misfortunes have overtaken us." They convinced the people and

they all agreed to eagerly approach the King who authorized them to practice the gentiles' observances. Just as we do today, go to church on SUNdays to worship our heavenly father in regard to the Roman God (Satan) on his so-called day of rest. We do it religiously! Our Father's Day of rest is the Sabbath, Saturday, day of worship. That hit me in my heart like a ton of bricks to write this. The irony, to find out the very thing that got us cursed, exiled and sent into punishment for, is the very thing we end up serving anyway.... pagan worship and on their God's day of rest!

Wow, how this rabbit hole goes so deep. It's filled with lies that took us right back where we were, at the point of being exiled from our homeland! Our Ancestors fought for their lives while trying to preserve our religion and way of life. That's a real reality shocker that we are Israel; and we always end up having this age-old fight where Esau wants to kill Jacob!

This is truly déjà vu for us, and we don't know it, how ironic. Because 'THIS' is 'THAT; what we are living in today being innocently killed just like at the time of exile from our homeland...Rome came into our homeland and attacked and killed us...this is that...that age old fight with Esau for power to rule! At that time some of the people outwardly chose to serve the pagan Gentile gods instead of standing for our God. They gave in to their enemy and became like them turning their backs on God. In present day time we are spiritually dead until our father resurrects us at the completion of our 400-year punishment, Eze 37. It will be our Spiritual Awakening!

Again Israel, we are faced with a choice of choosing life or death, free will, Deut. 30:15. For those of us who choose life will experience the reality of Deut. 28:1-14, 'The Blessings'. We will enjoy the blessing of being the head and not the tail. We will always be on top and never beneath. All nations will look at us and call us blessed.

Jacob has been hidden in the church, but we are taught that we are Christians and Gentiles. In the Apocryphal books, it identifies who the Gentiles are; just as Gen. 10:1-5, tells us that the Gentiles are Japheth's people. How can we be Gentiles and go into 400 years of punishment and not know our identity, or where we truly come from? The nations in Africa will tell you that you were not native of their lands. We migrated there between 70 A.D. to about 134 A.D., because of being exiled from our homeland. The nations in Africa (Ham) are still killing Jacob as well today. Sunday worshippers of today do not know who they are truly paying homage to on their day of worship. They forsake worship on the Sabbath day.

I'm here to correct that madness. If we look at the slave laws from the 1600's, you will know for certain that Christianity, Catholicism, and Muslim faiths were forced on us. We are none of those things. Our oppressors have us believing we are so many different things, and that the Jewish people are us. A prerequisite of being God's people is to go through the "Bread of Adversity" and the "Waters of Affliction," that were supposed to last 400 years according to scripture, Gen 15:13-14 and Acts 7:6. This is the curse of Deut. 28:15-68. In modern day times we are suffering "The Bread of Adversity" while the "Jews" are busy being greedy enslaving the world in debt! Catholic Rome (West) the church, is the other leg of the Jews. They both represent the Israelites and the church which belongs to God. Remember, they stole our ancestral history and replaced us as a nation. Overnight the Hebrew civilization became Gentile/white, I Maccabees 3:48. They made our history their his-story!

They locked us out of our own history and ancestral rites. The biggest trickery ever pulled on an unsuspecting people. We were never aware that another race of people would assimilate us as a people. The most ridiculous thing is, no one ever called them on this when they stole our identity.

The world is not that naive when there is documented history that proves this conversion happened. But no one asked why would they take a people's religion that their own God turned against them for? They saw wealth, and a powerful ancient heritage they could claim. They identified with Satan! They could not believe their eyes that black people had rich, cultured kingdoms. So, they decided to write us out of our own history and pretend as if we were never those people.

The Jewish people are converts to our religion and way of life. Their conversion started in the eighth century A.D., but this has been our way of life since our heavenly Father called our fore father Abraham in Gen. 15. We are the 'Chosen Seed'. The Jewish people true identity is Khazars. I go into detail about them in the chapter of "The Huns". Gen 9:27 says that Japhet will live in the tents of Shem and Canaan will be his servant. They made us the servants while they rule in havoc over us until our time is complete in 2019.

We are the chosen seed of the Most High YHWH. We came from Noah's son Shem (Gen. 10:22) thru Arphaxad, through Father Abraham. Our heavenly Father chose us out of all the people of the earth (Deut. 7:6/Acts 13:17).

This is who The Ancient of Days/God has made us to be in his image

- Inheritors- we are very wealthy
- Kings/Priest
- A powerful people
- Holy/Royal
- Supernatural beings, spiritual discerners
- Spiritual people; time does not affect us like other people
- People of the light
- We have dominion over earthly/spiritual realms
- Kingdom people

After Noah days, all spiritual light left the world and we became spiritually dead. We were chosen to be God's people but did not know our father. Our Ancestors didn't develop personal relationship with him because the people were afraid of our own Father. They relied on the priest to go to God for them.

At the time of our punishment when we were in our own land, Rome conquered Jerusalem in 134 A.D. The chapter of Luke 21 is telling us the city of Jerusalem would be surrounded and we  would be attacked. Our day of exile was upon us. We had to leave, fight or die, or be taken captive.

We had been warned by the prophets and disciples of our repetitive behavior in shedding each other's blood on the land, worshipping and sacrificing to idols, and our leaders/Pharisees being oppressors, extortionist, and spoilers of the poor, widow, and fatherless. Our women walked around proudly with loose morals wearing gold and tingling ankle bracelets on their feet, stumbling, because they were full of pride.

Our actions spoke louder than words. You could see our sins as clear as you saw Sodom's. We didn't care and didn't try to hide it. Our father turned his back and hid his face from us because of our disobedience. But he still has his hand stretched out to all those who want a personal relationship with him in Jesus.

With all this going on, our people forgot our covenant with our father. We were in a divorce situation with God. He said he would give us a decree of divorce, Isa 50:1. His "Day of Vengeance" sealed that for us as that dreadful day had finally crept up on us. We broke our end of the Covenant God made with our fathers. We had to leave our land

and suffer the repercussions of our decision.

Esau and the Huns

There are three powers that still want to kill Jacob, Satan, Esau, and the Gentiles. Esau is twin brother to Jacob/Israel. With Satan being the ultimate power over the other two, knows his time is short. He has to try and usurp God using as many people as he can to attain this. Esau vowed to kill Jacob for tricking him twice in one day out of his birth rite and the blessing. He's still killing us to this day. While we were going into exile, Esau blended in with the Romans and became one with them, Jasher 90:8. Last, is Japheth, Gen. 9:27 says, "God shall enlarge Japheth and he shall dwell in the tents of Shem; and Canaan shall be his servant.

What this mean is, Japheth is a humongous group of people spread out all over the world. Their claim is estimated to be about 15,500,000 Jews worldwide in today's time. They shall live in the tents of Shem means, they are posing as all the black nations of the Middle East...pretending to be the Children of Israel and the other black nations. Canaan will be their servant or slave; they made Shem's seed to become as Canaan and to serve as slaves. This curse was for Ham's grandson Canaan, not the twelve tribes of Israel through Shem.

Esau

Our ancient writ has a lot to say about Esau. The book of Genesis gives detailed accounts about Esau when he sells his birth-rite. But as we read, we find out in the book of Jasher 27:1-13 what Esau was up to before he encountered his twin brother Jacob, the birth-rite, and red pottage. Nimrod was a mighty hunter before God. He was still alive in the land in Esau's day. He saw Esau was just as skillful as he was in hunting; Nimrod became jealous in his heart. He and a couple of his men would lie in wait for Esau to observe him. Esau knew Nimrod and his men would watch him. He laid a plan in his heart to kill Nimrod. On this particular day Esau hunted Nimrod and the two men with him. Esau suddenly came upon Nimrod and cut off his head. A deadly battle ensued with Nimrod's two soldiers where Esau kills the two men. Esau took Nimrods garment because they were of great value.

Whoever wore them claimed dominion and a right to rule the earth. The garment was passed down to Noah, who was to give it to the promised inheritor "Jacob. "But Ham stole it when Noah was drunk and before he uncovered his Father's nakedness, meaning he made fun of his dad's necked drunken condition and Noah knew it. In Jasher 27, it tells us, Ham gave the garment to his son Cush. Cush gave it to Nimrod who became a mighty hunter in the earth. Nimrod wore the garment that God made for Adam. This is the garment of dominion and ruler ship which entitled him to be ruler of the world.

In Gen. 27:37 Isaac said this to Esau, "I have already made him your master; I have given him all his brothers as servants, I have given him grain and wine, to sustain him. So, what can I do for you my son? Then Esau cried father bless me, then his father spoke again saying, far from the richness of the earth and the dew of heaven above your home will be. By your sword you will live, and your brother will you serve. But when you win your freedom, you will shake his yoke off your neck.' In modern day times, Esau has claimed the whole world by the sword and keeps dominion with the use of the sword.

In Malachi 1:2-5 NJB, "I have loved you", says Yahweh. But you ask, "How have you shown your love?" Was not Esau Jacob's brother? Declares Yahweh; even so, I loved Jacob, but I hated Esau. I turned his mountains into a desert and his heritage into dwellings in the wastelands. If Edom says, "We have been struck down, but we shall rebuild our ruins," Yahweh Sabaoth says this, "Let them build, but I shall pull down! They will be known as the Land of Wickedness and Nation with which Yahweh is angry forever! You will see this yourselves and say, "Yahweh is mighty beyond the borders of Israel"

Esau gain control by becoming one with Rome when they were attacked and conquered in Jerusalem 70 a.d. to 134 a.d. Jerusalem fell; the Hebrews had to go into exile. Esau's land was conquered by Rome, as a result Esau became one with Chittim, Book of Jasher 90:8-9. What this means is Esau fulfilled his vow that he would rule the world supreme. But Esau's rule has an expiration date, just as our punishment of being exiled has an expiration date. Esau's Gentile rule is running short on time. They were always subject to our leadership. Through our fall, an opportunity was given to Satan to have ruler ship over the earth for a short time. Satan has his own people like God has his children. They are called "Serpent people." Remember Satan was a serpent in the Garden of Eden, and his people are of the same characteristics.

The Huns

The Huns went by many names depending on what country they were in. In Elam they were known as Parni, to the Parthians as Scythians or Arians, to China as Zhou, Anatolia as Dorians or Ionians. They originated in Central Asia. They were such a barbaric  people, that the Mongols drove them out of Central Asia. They divided into two groups. The one group's name is the Ottoman Turks who relocated to the region known as the Crimea. The second group were the Khazars. They relocated to the Caucasus Mountain area. In Arthur Koestler's book, "The Thirteenth Tribe" he accounts that the people that lived around the Huns, called them "serpent people", The Huns are the children of Satan.

Remember, The Huns are from Togarmah and Ashkenaz, who is Japheth's grandson through Gomer, Gen. 10:2. Cain's seed is wicked and goes against the will of God because Satan enticed him to use for his purpose and Cain accepted. Like Cain, the Huns had this same heart. The Khazars became Jews because they did not want to submit to being Christians under the authority of Rome, nor did they want to become Muslim under the authority of the Caliph whom the Ottoman Turks became. They were such an enormous amount of people that covered over a million miles of land that they did not want to commit sovereignty to anyone else. This was there start of conversion to becoming us.

Africa the Kingdom of Benin
~From the writing of Olaudah Equiano~

We went into the Benin area of Africa/Guinea from Senegal to Angola which included a variety of kingdoms. The Kingdom of Benin was massive. It was wealthy with richness and cultivated soil. It had a powerful king and warlike Hamites all around. It was situated right off the coast although the interior ran deep into Africa terminating at length by the Empire of Abyssinia 1500 miles from its beginning.

We were a people who honored marriage. Marriage was sacred among us and all of the nations of Africa. If anyone was caught in infidelity, they were given a death penalty or sometimes made a slave. We were a nation of dancers, musicians, and poets. We developed instruments of music. At celebrations all would participate in sections. The men would demonstrate a dance in an act of war. The married women were next. The young men would do their dance and lastly the maidens (unmarried women). Each dance depicting a scene of real life. Men and women wore pretty much the same type of clothing. A long calico or muslin wrapped loosely around the body. It was in the form of a highland plaid (Kente cloth?). It was usually dyed a bright, rich blue which was our favorite color. The color was extracted from berries.

Our women of distinction wore gold ornaments on their arms and legs. Women usually spin/weave cotton then dye it. They make it into garments. They also made earthen vessels and tobacco pipes. Our women were warriors. They were taught to use weapons of war.

Then Again (2016) "The Interesting Narrative of the Life of Olaudah Equiano" [PDF] Retrieved from http://www.thenagain.info/Classes/Sources/Equiano.html

Empress Em Sharon Yisrael

Yuchi war dance, illustration by Philip Georg Friedrich von Reck, Georgia, c. 1736

African American Native Americans

Yuchi war dance, illustration by Philip Georg Friedrich von Reck, Georgia, c. 1736

Transatlantic Slave Trade

We had been in the land of Benin close to 1500 years before the "Lord's Day of Vengeance was upon us in the various regions of Africa where we relocated. Transatlantic slave trade starts in 1502 but escalated by 1518 with thousands being sent each year to the Hispaniola. Christopher Columbus charted out the way for the transatlantic slave trade to take Africans to Hispaniola for sale. Black people became more precious than oil or gold. In 1619 a Dutch ship by the name of the White Lion captured 20 plus free Children of Israel from a Spanish ship that was on its way to Hispaniola.

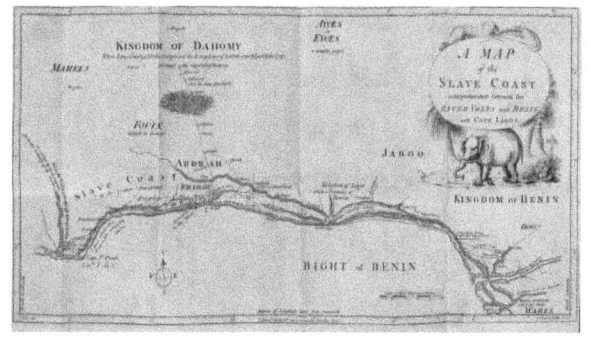

They were free until the White Lion captured them, detoured, and took them to Jamestown, Virginia to sell into the slave market. This was the start date that counts towards our 400 years of bondage in a strange land, Act 7:6, but let's see what the word says, about slavery:

Isa. 9:1-6, as the past humbled the land of Zebulun and the land of Naphtali, so the future will glorify the Way of the Sea, beyond the Jordan, the territory of the nations. The people that walk-in darkness have seen a great light on the inhabitants in the land of the shadow of death, upon them hath the light blazed forth.

2 You have enlarged the nation, you have increased its joy; they

rejoice before you as people rejoice at harvest time, as they exult when they are dividing spoils.

3 For the yoke that weighed on it; the bar across its shoulders; the rod of its oppressor, These you have broken as on the day of Midian,

4 For all the footgear clanking over the ground and all the clothing rolled in blood, will be burnt, will be food for the flames.

5 For unto us a son has been born for us, a son has been given to us, and dominion has been laid on his shoulders; and this is the name he has been given, 'Wonderful-Counselor, Mighty-God, Eternal Father, and Prince-of-Peace,'

6 to extend his dominion in boundless peace, over the throne of David and over his kingdom to make it secure and sustain it in fair judgment and integrity. From this time onwards and forever, the jealous love of Yahweh Sabaoth will do this.

As we can see these verses are talking about how our oppressors put shackles on our ancestor's necks and chains on their feet and hands. We have enlarged their nations when they brought us over into their lands. We were the harvest that they took great joy in dividing up as spoil among themselves at the slave auctions. The nations rejoiced over our enslavement in the land of the shadow of death. Jesus was given to us to ensure that the gifts of Kingship, Priesthood,

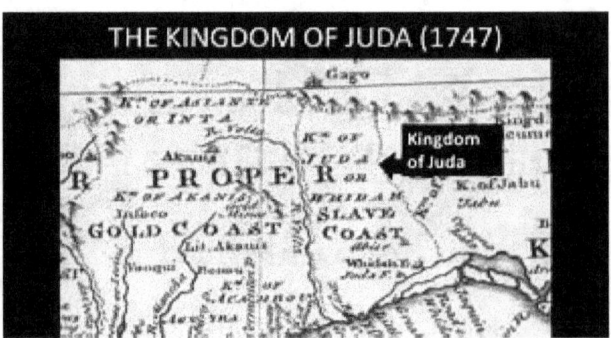

and Royalty, transfers back to us through the Kingdom of God being establish on earth again at the end of Gentile rule. These three were gifts given to our forefathers as a part of our inheritance which was passed down to the descendants. "We are the descendants, we are the Inheritors, the hidden ones."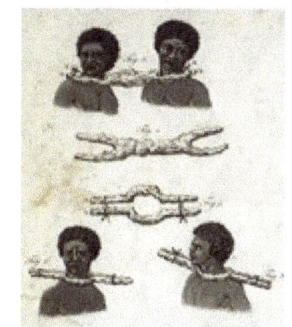
In the land of our exile, when he reveals us, God will show his light on us to tell the world that the modern-day Jews are imposters! We are people of the light! We are his and he is ours!

Arab Slavery

Islam conversion came in the 8th century B.C. to the Hamites of Africa by the black indigenous Arabs who are Shem. The modern-day Christian culture was hijacked by Esau from the ancient Babylonians and turned into a culture of wickedness. It is disguised as Christianity. The very same is true of modern-day Islam. The Turks hijacked and stole this religion from the true black Arabs and made it into today's Muslim faith known for radical terrorism.

Their beginning starts when the Seljuk Turk, Chief Toghril Beg went to Baghdad in December 1055 to seek permission to become a Sultan and offered his daughter's hand in marriage. The Arab Caliph al-Qa'im (who reigned 1031-75) enthroned him, and married his daughter, a Seljuk princess. This was the beginning of their downfall. Toghril then proclaimed himself sultan at Neyshabur in 1038.

The Ottoman Turks will be best remembered for supplanting themselves as the true Arabs who are Shem and a black people, for stealing their ancient religion, ancestral heritage and rites.

Most Arab tribes migrated into the Sudan in the 12th century a.d. and introduced Islam. Sudanese Arabs are migrants primarily from the Arabian Peninsula. This includes pre-existing indigenous populations of Sudan that are predominantly Nubian people who also share a common history with Egypt. In addition, a few Arabian tribes existed in Sudan prior to the advent of Islam. These were Shem's Arab who is

Ishmael. He is Abraham's son by Hagar.

The bible speaks about Ishmael in Gen 16:12. It says Ishmael will be a wild donkey of a man, his hand will be against every man and their hand against him, and he will live in hostility towards all his brothers. Ishmael's descendants were responsible for converting some of us to Islam while in the land of Africa before slavery. During slavery, the Arabs helped the slave traders capture us.

In Jerusalem, Muslim temples are built throughout Israel. Ishmael built his Muslim Temple on the Temple mount to declare his right as the eldest son of Abraham. He desires to rule the world. It is still there at present in modern day time.

Our heavenly father Yahweh always uses the older to serve the younger. He promotes the younger to a place of authority and position. This is something that the world can't grasp and does not understand. God don't use seniority status like man does; he chooses a different method. Even though there are nations connected to the chosen people through Ham and Shem, they are counterfeits, and therefore disqualified to inherit the promise.

The original modern-day Arabs are in Yemen. Some migrated to Syria, Iraq, and Lebanon. They were hidden as well. All Semitic black kingdoms lost power and control over their land and ancient heritage.

https://en.wikipedia.org/wiki/Sudanese_Arabs

[1] Here is a timeline of the Ottoman Turks rise to power and the enslavement of the "Black Lands

Date	Event
1300 A.D.	**Osman leads the way (About 1300 A.D.).** To help win a major battle, Osman leads his troops and displaces the Seljuk Turks. He becomes the leader of the new Ottoman dynasty.
1326 A.D.	**A new capital.** Osman and his troops lay siege to the city of Bursa in northwest Turkey. When the city falls, Bursa is made into the capital of the Ottoman Empire. Osman dies in 1326.
1326 A.D.	**Family line continues (1326 - 1389 A.D.).** Osman's son, Orhan, rules after his father's death. He gains control of Thrace in 1345. His son Murad I rules next. He sets up the system to train ex-slaves into elite soldiers known as Janissaries. He dies in the battlefield while defeating the Serbians.
1400	**A win and a loss (1400 - 1402 A.D.).**

---

[1] http://www.realhistoryww.com/world_history/ancient/Misc/True_Negros/The_True_Negro_2.htm

A.D.	Bayezid extends the empire from the Danube River in Bulgaria to the Euphrates River in the east. Mongolian raiders crush his troops in Turkey in 1402 and take him prisoner. Bayezid dies within the year, and the Ottoman Empire is split among his sons.
1402 A.D.	**Civil war, then victory (1402 – 1413 A.D.).** Bayezid's sons fight for control. In 1413 Mehmed wins and reunites the empire. He dies in 1421.
1453 A.D.	**The end of the Byzantine Empire.** Mehmed II lays siege to the Byzantine capital of Constantinople in 1453. He uses siege guns and bombards the walls for eight weeks. Heavy fighting continues, but the Byzantine capital is defeated when Emperor Constantine XI dies in battle. The city is now called Istanbul.
1453 A.D.	**Ottoman culture flourishes (1453 – 1481 A.D.).** Mehmed II rules for thirty years. During his reign Istanbul becomes a political, cultural, and economic center. Mosques, bazaars, roads, inns, and baths are built. A special tax is now charged to non-Muslim residents.

1520 A.D.	**Suleiman I reigns (1520 – 1566 A.D.)** One of the best known and most powerful leaders of the empire is Suleiman I, known as Suleiman the Magnificent. He conquers parts of western Asia and southeast Europe in his desire to convert people to Islam. The Ottoman Empire reaches its peak under his rule.
1566 A.D.	**A slow decline (1566 – 1574 A.D.)** At Suleiman I's death, his son Selim II rules. However, he is not like his father. He never goes to fight battles and his government is unstable. During his reign the Turkish fleet is smashed at the Battle of Lepanto in Greece.
1606 A.D.	**At odds with Persia (1606 – 1639 A.D.)** Poor leaders continue, reducing the Ottoman threat upon the European world. Fighting begins with the Persians and continues until 1639. The Turks, however, do capture Crete from the Venetians in that year.
1683 A.D.	**A losing battle.** The Ottomans try to conquer Venice in 1683 but fail. In 1697, as Austrian troops push into the Ottoman territory in Hungary, the Turks are defeated at Zenta. To keep peace the Turks give up much of their land in that region.

1821 A.D.	**Greece revolts.** Starting in 1821, Greece revolts against the Ottomans. A long struggle ensues with the Greeks eventually getting help from Britain, France, and Russia. They win their independence in 1830.
1878 A.D.	**More losses.** Abdul Hamit II tries to instill reforms into the empire, including adding a constitution and a parliament. These reforms fail, however. In 1878 the Congress of Berlin acknowledges the independence of Serbia, Romania, and Bulgaria.
1912 A.D.	**The Balkan Wars (1912 - 1913 A.D.)** Though actually two different battles, the goal of the Balkan Wars is to take over the European lands that belong to the Ottoman Empire. Its efforts are successful.
1914 A.D.	**The end of a war and an empire (1914 - 1923 A.D.).** During World War I, the Ottoman Empire sides with the Central Powers. They lose the war, and peace treaties cause the empire to dissolve. The Republic of Turkey is established in 1923. Although in power for over 600 years, the Ottoman Empire will best be remembered for its glory years of strong

> leadership and cultural influences that affected the lands they conquered.

THE TURKS TAKE CONTROL OF ARABIA

The Turks first started usurping the Arabs when the Seljuq Turk chief Toghril Beg proclaimed himself sultan at Neyshabur in 1038. Toghril entered Baghdad in December 1055, and the Arab caliph al-Qa'im (reigned 1031–75) enthroned him and married a Seljuq princess.

The Turks took direct control of Arabia when Sultan Mahmud II (1808-39), ordered his viceroy/governor of Egypt, the Turkic Albanian Muhammad Ali, to send an expedition to Arabia: which between 1811 and 1813 expelled the Arab Wahhabis from the Hejaz. In a further campaign (1816-18), Ibrahim Pasha, the viceroy's eldest son, defeated the Wahhabis in their homeland of Najd, and brought central Arabia under Albanian control.

After World War I, Blacks in the Turkish ruled lands, have their identities stolen by the Turks, and their Mulattoes, after the break-up of the Ottoman Empire. As with the Berbers, Egyptians, etc. After the breakup of the Ottoman Empire after WWI, and the granting of independence to those countries after WWII, The Arabs saw their identity stolen by Whites (mainly Turks and their mulattoes) and other mixed-race people.

Thus, Egypt is "The Arab Republic of Egypt" Syria is "The Syrian

Arab Republic" Libya is "The Great Socialist People's Libyan Arab Jamahiriya" Jordan is "The Hashemite Kingdom of Jordan" (Hashemite is the Latinate version of the Arabic transliteration of Hāšimī) and traditionally refers to those belonging to the Banu Hashim Arabs, or "clan of Hashim", a clan within the larger Arab Quraish tribe. It also refers to an Arab dynasty whose original strength stemmed from the network of tribal alliances and blood loyalties in the Hejaz region of Arabia, along the Red Sea. (One can only wonder how sparsely populated Arabia could have possibly produced all of those people - what nonsense)!

In 1820-21 Muhammad Ali sent an expedition up the Nile and conquered much of what is now the northern Sudan. By so doing, he made himself master of one of the principal channels of the slave trade and began an African Empire that was to be expanded under his successors. The conquest of the Sudan was intended to provide recruits. But the slaves, encamped at Aswan, died wholesale, and Muhammad Ali had to look elsewhere for his troops. In 1823 he took to conscripting Egyptian peasants for the rank and file of his new army. On the other hand, the officers were mostly Turkish Ottomans, while the director of the whole enterprise, Sulayman Pasha (Colonel Sève), was a former French officer. The conscription was brutally administered. In 1882 the British once again invaded and occupied Egypt. This occupation was to last until the end of WWI. After which, Egypt became a protectorate of Britain.

http://www.realhistoryww.com/world_history/ancient/Misc/True_Negros/The_True_Negro_2.htm

Black Kings the Northern Tribes (Jacobites)

Only one can truly be an Arab

Up to the late 1600's Great Britain and Europe was ruled by the black Northern kingdoms of Israel. They had been in these lands since their exile around 721 b.c. before it became inhabited. During this Renaissance period Gentile rule began This is how Europe went dark. A paradigm shift took place that transferred power to Esau to rule Satan's kingdom for 400 years. The first became last! I have included their coats of arms in the back of the book under the picture section

TIMELINE FOR THE THIRTY YEARS' WAR, 1618-1648

1590	The militant Catholic Habsburg Archduke Ferdinand (Emperor Ferdinand II, 1619-1637) stamps out Protestantism in Austria, while Duke Maximilian (reigned 1597-1651) does the same in Bavaria.
1607	After religious riots in the Free City of Donauwörth, the Emperor authorizes Bavaria to occupy the city and impose Catholicism. Protestants walk out of the Reichstag in 1608, and the institutions of the Holy Roman Empire are paralyzed. Arms race between the

	"Protestant Union" led by the Palatinate and the "Catholic League" led by Bavaria.
1609	12 Years' Truce between Spain and the United Provinces; succession crisis in the strategic Rhineland duchies of Cleves, Jülich, and Berg, which are claimed both by a Catholic and by the Protestant Elector of Brandenburg.
1610	Militant Calvinist Frederick V becomes Elector of the Palatinate (1610-36); he and his advisor, Anhalt, seek to persuade all Protestants that a vast Catholic conspiracy aims at the forcible suppression of Protestantism everywhere.
1618	Habsburg Archduke Ferdinand provokes rebellion when he attempts to stamp out Protestantism in Bohemia; the Defenestration of Prague.
1619	Grand alliance forms of Emperor Ferdinand II, his cousin, King Philip III of Spain, and Duke Maximilian of Bavaria. Bohemians elect Frederick V, the Elector of the Palatinate, as their king but can find no other Protestant allies.
1620	Habsburg forces crush the Bohemians at the Battle of White Mountain.

1621	War resumes between the Spanish and Dutch.
1621-23	Bavaria completes conquest of the Palatinate; Maximilian assumes Frederick's title as Elector. (Simplicissimus is born soon after the Protestant defeat at the Battle of Höchst, June 1622.)
1625-1628	King Christian IV of Denmark intervenes to defend German Protestants, but the much larger Catholic armies of Wallenstein (Imperial) and Tilly (Bavarian) fight their way to the Baltic coast and crush all Protestant resistance.
1629	Emperor Ferdinand II issues Edict of Restitution, ordering the return to Catholic control of all bishoprics and monasteries secularized since 1552.
1630-1632	King Gustavus Adolphus of Sweden invades Germany and fights his way to Munich before dying in battle.
1633	Cardinal Richelieu provides Sweden with massive subsidies to keep it in the war, and French troops invade Lorraine (inspiring the series of woodcuts by Jacques Callot, *The Miseries of War*).
1634	The Imperial & Bavarian armies inflict a crushing

	defeat on the Swedes and Saxons at the Battle of Nördlingen, September 6, 1634. (Simplicissimus emerges from his hermit's lair to enter the world.)
1635	The Peace of Prague: Ferdinand II greatly weakens terms of Edict of Restitution to achieve reconciliation with the Protestant Electors of Saxony & Brandenburg. Thereafter the war basically pits Austria and Spain against France and Sweden, but it continues to be fought on German soil.
1640	Collapse of Spanish military power as Catalonia and Portugal revolt.
1643	Louis XIII dies, and the HABSBURG princess Anne of Austria becomes regent (while Cardinal Mazarin succeeds Richelieu), but France's anti-Habsburg policy remains unchanged; peace talks begin in Westphalian cities of Münster & Osnabrück.
1645	Swedes achieve a knockout punch against Imperial army at Battle of Jankov in Bohemia, March 6, 1645.
1646	Dutch delegation arrives at peace talks, which become truly comprehensive.
1648	In the final Peace of Westphalia, every contender gain

something, as all parties agree on the need for a "balance of power." The Habsburgs drop the Edict of Restitution, while the Swedes drop the issue of toleration for Protestants in Austria and Bohemia. Calvinists gain the same rights granted Lutherans and Catholics in the Peace of Augsburg in 1555: "Whoever rules, his religion."

Here are some pictures that explain how Japheth's nations came and took over. Gentile rule started when they conquered The United Kingdom of Great Britain and Europe in the 1600's. This is what happened to the Northern Tribes of Israel who were the Emperors, Empresses, Kings, Queens, and Royalty...they were killed and the majority went into slavery in Hispaniola and the West Indies.

30 Years War picture 1590 to 1648

A lot of these pictures have been whitenized.

Manuscript Minatures from the Wenzel Bible 1389

Empress Em Sharon Yisrael

Trees of Righteousness/Fulfillment of the Curses of Deuteronomy 28

Illumination from the German Wenceslaus/Wenzel Bible of 1389:
(Old Testament translation).

Illumination from the German Wenceslaus/Wenzel Bible of 1389:
(Old Testament translation).

Partially Whitenized painting of the death of Roland at the Battle of Roncevaux: by Jean Fouquet (1420-1480). From an illustrated manuscript of the 15th century.

Illumination from the German Wenceslaus/Wenzel Bible of 1389; (Old Testament translation).

Stephen I defeats Kean, Duke of the Bulgarians and Slavs: Chronicon Pictum, before 1360.

Trees of Righteousness/Fulfillment of the Curses of Deuteronomy 28

Notice the flag being taken down of the black king in green.

The Hapsburg Family

Empress Em Sharon Yisrael

Illustration from unknown Illuminated Manuscript titled "Blessed Charlemagne in war against the Moors". In this Albino forgery, the dark pigment has been removed from the faces of the Knights on the left, to make it appear that Charlemagne and his soldiers were Albinos, and that they are attacking a Moor fort.

But note that the soldiers in the fort are wearing the exact "SAME" uniform as those approaching on Horseback. They are BOTH Europeans and are both wearing "CHAIN-MAIL" (Moors did not wear chainmail uniforms). Also note that the Fort "GATE" has been lifted to allow those coming on horseback "ENTRY" into the fort. Note that there is a Moor being held prisoner in a cell below (identified by his headband), but he is also wearing chainmail: suggesting that he may be a spy.

Our Present Condition – Dreg of the Cup of Trembling

I am sharing this from Facebook. This is a true depiction of who we are as a people because of the curses of Deut. 28:15-68. These adversities and afflictions still plague us as a people. What is missing from this excerpt is, the curse we are living in today has an end date! Mind you, their turn is next as scripture confirms. The ones that God allow to remain on the earth will experience worse conditions than we lived through when God punished us. They forgot to read what their end holds for them as well. They will reap what they have sown throughout our captivity. It has not been taught to us who we are as a people, so we are blind to what will happen to us.

A White man said: "BLACK PEOPLE ARE STILL OUR SLAVES". We can continue to reap profits from them without the effort of physical slavery. Their IGNORANCE is the primary weapon of containment. A great man once said, 'The best way to hide something from Black people, is to put it in a book.' They have the opportunity to read any book on any subject through the efforts of their fight for freedom, yet they refuse to read. Few read consistently, if at all. GREED is another weapon of containment. Last year Blacks spent 10 billion dollars during Christmas, out of their 450 billion dollars in total yearly income (2.22%). We can use them as our target market, for any business venture we care to dream up, they will buy into it.

They function totally by greed, disrespecting their own friends and families. They continually want more, and hardly save. They'd rather buy new sneakers, name brand shoes, nails and hair rather than invest in a business or a home. Some neglect their children to have the latest Michaels Jordan and Kors. Plus, they still think that having a Mercedes, gives them 'Status'. They're fools! A vast majority of them are still in poverty because of their greed is holding them back from making better communities. With the help of BET and the rest of their black media that often show destructive images into their own homes, we will continue to see huge profits like those of Tommy and Nike. Hilfiger has even jeered them, saying he doesn't want their money, and look at how the fools spend more with him than ever before!

They'll continue to show off to each other while White communities improve with the profits from our businesses that we market to them. SELFISHNESS is one of the major ways the (3%) "Three percent of the WORLD" continues to contain them. There are segments of their culture that has achieved some 'form' of success, but they didn't read that the talented 10% was responsible to aid The Non-Talented 90% in achieving a better life. Instead, that segment has created another class that looks down on their people or aids them in a condescending manner. Their selfishness does not allow them to be able to work together on any project of substance. When they do get together, their egos get in the way of their goal.

Their so-called help organizations seem to only want to promote their name without making any real change in their community. They are content to sit in conferences & conventions in our hotels, and talk about what they will do, while they award plaques to the best speaker not the best doer. They refuse to see that Together Each Achieves More

(TEAM). They do not understand that they are no better than each other because of what they own, as a matter of fact, most of them are but one or two paychecks away from poverty. All of which is under the control of our pens in our offices and our rooms. Yes, we will continue to contain them as long as they refuse to read, continue to buy anything they want, and keep thinking they are 'helping' their communities by paying dues to organizations which do little other than hold conventions in our hotels. By the way, don't worry about any of them reading this. THEY DON'T READ!"

We MUST rise from this post-traumatic slavery disorder.

My comment to this is that they should be aware of the traps they set for us; because the fury that Daddy God has for them will be unbearable. Our father will not allow them to keep their foot on our necks for long. This thing has a date to end. Seems they forgot about that! They looked upon our curse and punishment and thought to add insult to injury. The tables are turning. The first becomes last, will they feel this way about themselves? Will they like the world to look upon them as the scourge of the earth? What are they going to do? How will they handle it? Our heavenly father is jealous for us. He will not allow them to go unpunished. In fact, he said he will visit them before he brings us out from among them. We are witnessing the most powerful display of our Father's anger in natural disasters back to back! When we come out of our punishment, the Gentiles will go into their punishment.

Empress Em Sharon Yisrael

Christianity

Our pastors and leaders got this thing all twisted. Esau has gone to great lengths to trick you Jacob...he still wishes to kill you...he does not want you to inherit the blessings our heavenly father promised us. It is now taught in Theology, 'A Replacement Theology'. The church has replaced Israel. This is blasphemous! Who has bewitched you? I hope you all are not buying this, the first scripture that comes to mind in opposition to this is Rom. 11:17-24. There is a warning in that scripture that says, do not think the natural branches were broken off, so you could replace them without them being grafted back in again? You are in error thinking the church replaces the Children of Israel. For if God spared not the natural branches, take heed lest he also spare not thee, and verse 21. God made a perpetual covenant with Abraham, an oath to Isaac and confirmed the same to Jacob for a law, and also to Israel for an everlasting covenant, I Chronicles 16:15-18. Yahweh has always said throughout scripture that he would restore Jacob back to our homeland, Rom. 11:5. The world believes the Jews/Khazars are us. They are the wrong people. They are imposters.

We are black people whose ancestors came from Jerusalem by way of Benin, Africa, and the Slave Coast. Our people went through the horror and terror of slavery. We are enduring the "Bread of Adversity" (being black in America and wherever we have been scattered) and "The Waters of Affliction" (in the bellies of slave ships). Why on God's green earth would our pastors believe that we are

Gentiles and Christians? Our leaders have us believing we are any type of religion other than what we truly are, Hebrew bible believers "In the Way". Our worship day is supposed to be on Saturday not Sunday. So many of our people fought down through the ages to prevent the Sunday worship, but we accept it without question. The Hebrews and true church believers were persecuted for believing and worshipping the true way. When we gained our freedom, we freely accepted with open arms pagan's day of worship disguised as the true day of worship.

All religion and all churches come under the Maritime Admiralty Law of Rome. They belong to the pagan system of Rome. On Sunday you are showing respect to the Sun God Jupiter or Apollo (Satan), Rome's God day of rest.

Pagan Worship

When Rome captured Jerusalem around 70 ad, they broke into the Temple of The Most High God and defiled it with the abomination of the desolation. They setup the statute of their God Apollo/Jupiter who is really Satan in the place where the Ark of the Covenant sat. But of course, the Ancient of Days our heavenly father had the Ethiopian brothers in the way to come and take the Ark for safekeeping. During this time Esau became one with Kittim (Rome). Rome eventually took the Hebrew way of believing and called it Christianity in service to their God Apollo. Sunday was set aside as a rest day for him. No longer was it popular or lawful to worship on Saturdays. We were persecuted and killed for our wholesome way of life and worshipping in our faith whenever we were caught. This included circumcision of our boys according to God's word, and keeping the Sabbath, both of which were abolished. Our faith was a way of life. It allowed us to openly express our freedom of worship to our father and keeping his Law before Satan's authority began to rule in Jerusalem. We were killed because this violated Esau/Rome's new laws.

The Divided church

The Byzantine Empire was black and predominantly Greek speaking. They came from Antiquity into the middle ages. They were a part of the Afro-Eurasia continent under black rulership. Constantine came into ruler ship, he moved the Capital city to Constantinople (modern day Istanbul), originally known as Byzantium Eastern half of the Roman Empire. It fragmented and collapsed the Western Roman Empire. The Byzantium Eastern Roman Empire thrived for 1000 years more and then fell to the Ottoman Turks in 1453.

East/West schism of 1054 known as the Great Schism which divided the state church of the Roman Empire into Eastern (Greek) and Western (Latin branches which later became known as the Eastern Orthodox Church and the Roman Catholic Church). East and West relationship was embittered by political and ecclesiastical difference and theological disputes. Eastern Orthodox Church at present still shows the original Christians as they really were, (but whitenized) black people. The churches in the book of Revelation are the same churches that were in Antiquity in the medieval age when Gentile rule stated taking control. Rome fell around 476 a d when the German Odoacer dethroned the last King. He was the first barbarian to rule Rome. Catholic Rome wanted control over religion.

It was time for Gentile rule in religion to control the world. Today there are three main religions that controlled the world at large; Judaism, Christianity, and Muslim. Each wants world domination. Domination was given to us through our ancestors into antiquity! We have three gifts God gave our forefathers: the promise of Kingship, Priesthood, and Royalty. Our stolen history reflects this. This is why Jesus will take ruler ship of the earth and restore the three gifts back to us again. Dan. 7:21-22, 25-27 says, 21 "I beheld, and the same horn made war with the saints, and prevailed against them. 22 Until the Ancient of days came, and judgement was given to the saints of the Most High; and the time came that the saints possessed the kingdom. 25 And he shall speak great words against the Most High and shall wear out the saints of the Most High and think to change times and laws: and they shall be given into his hand until a time and times and the dividing of time. 26 But the judgement shall sit, and they shall take away his dominion, to consume and to destroy it unto the end. 27 And the kingdom and dominion, and the greatness of the kingdom is an everlasting kingdom, and all dominions shall serve and obey him.

Now check this carefully. We are the only people on the face of the planet that are hunted and killed without a cause, especially by the police or government military worldwide! No matter wherever we have been scattered in the world, there is no advocate to stand for us as a dispersed, exiled people. All other nations have an advocate, but we are left unprotected. In Daniel 7:21 the horn that is prevailing against us is now wearing us out by killing and rising up against us, while loathing us, because we are standing up for ourselves. They don't respect black lives, so to them, black lives don't matter because we are under a perpetual curse. The President (45) and Steve Bannon have colluded and come in agreement to take America back for themselves. After all, their ancestors raped, stole, and killed to take this land from the indigenous people. It has been prophesied that Esau (Japheth) would live by the sword and subdue the world. This is why God loves Jacob but hates Esau. Esau lives under the power of evil through Satan and rules through wickedness.

Empress Em Sharon Yisrael

Daddy, God's Love for Us

Our Heavenly Father loved us so much that he chose us as his family, Psalm 135:4/Amos 3:1-2/I Chron. 16:13. We are the original Judeans, the Tribe of Judah. In Psalm 83, tells us the nations came together and conspired to hide us and cut us off from being a nation; He has redeemed us from the curse and punishment of Deut. 28:15-68 He formed us for himself to show forth his praise, Isa. 43:21. In Eze. 16, God tells us how he found us as a newborn that was cast out in an open field left to die. Our father was an Amorite and out mother a Hittite. The birth of our nativity was of the land of Canaan. Our navel was not cut neither were we washed in water to be cleansed. We were not salted or swaddled.

No one pitied us which the same is our situation today, to do any of these things to have compassion on us. We were disgust in the day we were born. But when God passed by and saw us polluted in our own blood, he said to us LIVE! He washed us with water thoroughly to cleanse the blood from us and then anointed us with oil. He caused us to multiply as the bud of the field. He caused us to increase and become great. He made us very attractive. Our breast was fashioned and our hair grew where as we were naked and bare. When he passed by us, and looked upon us, it was a time of love. Daddy God spread his skirt over us and covered our nakedness. He clothed us with embroidered work, seal skins, fine linens, and silk.

He swore unto us and entered into a covenant with us; we became his. He decked us with ornaments by putting bracelets and chains on our necks. He put a jewel on our foreheads, earrings in our ears, and a beautiful crown upon our head. We were decked out in gold and silver. We did not eat anything but the best, flour, honey, and oil. We were exceedingly beautiful and did prosper into a kingdom. Our fame spread to the heathen because of our beauty. Our beauty was perfect through Daddy God's comeliness which he put on us. But we trusted in our good looks and played the harlot because of our fame. We fornicated with everyone that passed by. The garments God gave us, we used to decorate the pagan shrines.

We fell. We committed whoredom with the nations. We broke our father's covenant he made with us. Daddy God promised that his day of vengeance will come upon us. Daddy God said he would judge us as women that break wedlock and shed blood are judged. He gave us blood in fury and jealousy. He would cause us to cease from playing a harlot where we would no longer prostitute ourselves with the nations. He caused his fury to rest against us and his jealousy to depart. He said he would be quiet and will no more be angry with us which is our situation today. He remembers his covenant with us, I Chronicles 16:16-17.

Daddy God said he scattered us among the heathen according to our ways and our doings he judged us, Eze. 36:19-32. He says wherever he scattered us we profaned his holy name. But he took pity for his holy name and redeemed us for his name's sake. He will sanctify his great name in us before their eyes. He will take us from the heathen and gather us out of all the countries and bring us into our own land. He will then sprinkle clean water on us and we will be clean from all of our filthiness and all of our idols. He will give us a new heart and a new spirit. He will remove the stony heart from our flesh. He will cause us to walk in his statutes and we will keep his judgment to do them. We will dwell in the land he gave to our fathers. We will be his people and he will be our God.

Valley of the Dry Bones

Isa. 29:10 For the Lord hath poured out on you the spirit of deep sleep and hath closed your eyes, the prophets and your leaders the seers hath he covered. There is darkness in the world concerning who we are as a people. Of all the nations of people on the earth, we were stripped of our identity, our language, exiled from our homeland, stripped of our ancient heritage and culture. We forgot who we were. We became the base things of the world; we were laid flat even with the ground. Isaiah 51:23 says," But I will put it into the hands of them that afflict thee; who have said to thy soul, bow down, that we may go over: and thou hast laid thy body as the ground, and as the street, to them that went over. This is where we rank in the world...no matter how affluent you are this invisible mark of the curse is on us until we are released. Scriptures say we had to be punished as a fulfillment of prophecy. What is happening to us now, is our ancient heritage is being lived out by imposters.

In the chapter of Eze. 37 it tells us what will still happen to us as Yahweh's people. He's calling us back home to our own land to be with him and King Jesus our Messiah when he returns. The curse of Deut. 28 was only supposed to last 400 years. Time started counting towards our 400 years in 1619. 2019 completes that 400 years. The calendar was changed from the Hebrew ten-month year to Romulus twelve-month year. Our time is winding down fast. It was not a permanent sentence, but punishment to bring us back into correct relationship with him. He says he chastise those whom he loves. We are on course, set to be released from the curses of Deut 28. Our exile will be over. Gen. 15:13-14/Acts 7:6 both confirms this. We can find examples of what to expect when Jubilee occurs in the bible. After all, this is not the first time we had been in captivity. The Word promises it will be our last time to ever experience separation and death from our Father for disobedience.

Our pastors have not taught this to our people. They are under the belief that they are Christians and Gentiles who teach us these same misconceptions. They are our spiritual leaders, Shepherds over our souls. Don't you think they should have taught us about slavery since it only affects us as a people? Everybody wants to run away from the subject of slavery instead of learning more about how it was to affect us according to the bible. None of us knew that the perpetual curse of Deut. 28 has a date to end. It was right in our faces all the time when we read the bible.

We never knew the bible was specifically speaking to us as an exiled people. We let the world tell us who we were and are now, instead of opening the bible and finding ourselves. Every nation of people has their own nation and language they can identify with and go back to according to Genesis chapter 10. We are the only people on the face of the planet without a language and an identifiable nation. They say you came from Africa but what part? Even the people of that land will tell you that you were a foreigner. That is not our homeland. It is true we are from Africa, Northeast Africa, in the land of Israel, city of Jerusalem, which in Modern-day times is called the Middle East. We are Judah here in North America. Some of the ten tribes are in South and Central America and their islands, and Benjamin is in South Africa.

When darkness came over us, we forgot who we were. We are still clueless to this very day. In the book of Eze.37, Yahweh is telling Ezekiel to prophesy to the dry bones so that they can live. In verse eleven, Yahweh put sinew and flesh on the bones, but the bones say, "Our bones are dry our hope has gone; we are done for." Verse twelve, "So prophecy, say to them, "The Lord Yahweh says this: I am now going to open your graves; I shall raise you from your graves, my people, and lead you back to the soil of Israel. And you will know that I am Yahweh, when I open your graves and raise you from your graves my people, and put my spirit in you, and you revive, and I resettle you on your own soil. Then you will know that I, Yahweh, have spoken and done this-declares the Lord Yahweh."

Next, he had Ezekiel to take two sticks, one for the House of Judah to write on and one for the House of Ephraim. He told Ezekiel to join the two sticks together and make them one. He will take the Israelites from the nations where they have gone. He will gather them together from everywhere and bring them home to their own soil. He will make us into one nation in the country on the mountain of Israel. There will be one King that will reign over us, King Jesus. He will give us a new heart and a new spirit that we may never turn against him again. He shall make an eternal covenant with us to be our God and we will be his people. He will resettle us and make us grow as a people again. The entire world will know Yahweh the sanctifier of Israel when his sanctuary is with us forever.

"Valley of the dry bones" mean our ancestors and recent dead that are in the four corners of the earth will be awakened with new flesh and spirit. They will get up out of their graves and leave those lands. It will be a time like no other in the earth.

Only a remnant is returning back to our homeland. The President of the United States has sold us out to the Alt Right and declared a race war against us to 'Make America Great Again.' Only a remnant will survive this war, 12,000 per tribe worldwide, Rev. 7:1-3-8. Daddy God, Yahweh Sabaoth, the God of War is coming to get us with his hosts of Angelic armies. We are going to the Wilderness of Nations where the Lord will plead with us face to face Eze.20:35. He said there, he will give us a new heart and a new spirit Eze.36:26.

JUBILEE

Isaiah 60:1-2 says, "Arise, shine, for thy light is come, and the glory of the Lord is risen upon thee. For behold, the darkness shall cover the earth, and gross darkness the people: but the Lord shall arise upon thee, and his glory shall be seen upon thee." This passage of scripture means that all slave descendants and Israelites worldwide will light up, the very same way Moses did when he went up on the mountaintop and came back down with his face illuminated. That is how Yahweh will show the world who his true children are. No more distorted his-story filled with lies from a people who are posing as us. The world will know the truth, and we will confirm the truth about ourselves with our appearance. This glow cannot be duplicated with a spray tan!

Darkness means there is no knowledge of who we are in the world, to ourselves or to the Gentiles. Yahweh will rise on you; the brightness of our pineal gland will burst forth and illuminate us. When our illumination takes place, the Gentiles will come to witness the brightness of our rising. Our children and every Hebrew who are caught up in the system worldwide must return back to our homeland. Daddy Yahweh Sabaoth and Jesus the Messiah request our presence back into the homeland of our inheritance, Canaan. Verse 5 tells us that at the sight of seeing our sons and daughters being brought to us, our hearts will throb and dilate, since the riches of the sea will flow to us, and the wealth of the nations is coming to us.

Well how are we supposed to get back to our homeland you ask? Verse 8-9 says," Who are these flying like a cloud, like doves to their dovecote? Why, the coasts and islands put their hope in me and the vessels of Tarshish take the lead in bringing your children from far away and their silver and gold with them for the sake of the name of

Yahweh your God. Here is your answer. Our father is bringing us home in airplanes and ships. Jewish encyclopedia.com says the ships of Tarshish are any large vessel capable of making long sea journeys. These will be first class, luxurious Flights and cruises fit for royalty.

For the whole creation waits for the Sons of God to be revealed, Romans 8:19 is connected to Isa. 60:1-2 and Eze. 36. Yahweh has a purpose for the earth when we are revealed. When the revealing happens, we become illuminated. The land of Israel our mother has to start reproducing again to support us when we go back into her. In Ezekiel 36 Yahweh tells the mountains and land to produce. He even gives the animals a sense of peace for them not to harm us. Yahweh tells Ezekiel to prophesy to the mountains of Israel and say, "Mountains of Israel, hear the word of Yahweh.

The Lord Yahweh says this: Since the enemy has gloated over you by saying: Aha! These eternal heights are owned by us now, very well, prophesy! Say: The Lord Yahweh says this: Since you have been ravaged and seized on from all sides and have become the property of the rest of the nations, and become the subject of people's talk and gossip, very well, mountains of Israel, hear the word of the Lord Yahweh! The Lord Yahweh says this to the mountains and hills, to the ravines and valleys, to the devastated ruins and abandoned cities which have been put to the sack and have become a laughing-stock to the rest of the nations all round; very well, the Lord Yahweh says this: I am speaking to the rest of the nations and to the whole of Edom who so exultantly and contemptuously took possession of my country to despoil its pastureland."

Because of this prophecy about the land of Israel, Say to the mountains and hills, to the ravines and valleys, "The Lord Yahweh says this: I am speaking in my jealousy and rage; because you are enduring the insults of the nations, very well, the Lord Yahweh says this: I raise my hand and I swear that the nations all around you shall have their own insults to bear. "Mountains of Israel, you will grow branches and bear fruit for my people Israel, who will soon return. Yes, I am coming to you, I shall turn to you; you will be tilled and sown. I shall increase your population, the whole House of Israel, yes, all. The cities will be inhabited, and the ruins rebuilt. I shall increase your population, both human and animal; they will be fertile and reproduce. I shall repopulate you as you were before; I shall make you more prosperous than you were before, and you will be their heritage, and never again will you rob them of their children. This is what we have to look forward to when we go into our homeland to re-inhabit it. The Jewish posers who are in our land now did not benefit from any of these things.

The land did not produce for them nor did they light up the way he will illuminate us. You have just read what our Abba has said about us being revealed and re-inhabiting our land. They say they are the real Children of Israel, if this is true, why didn't they experience the 400-year curse/punishment? Their Holocaust was only four years of suffering they brought on themselves by trying to appear to fulfill scripture. God said 400 years, not 4 years. What is four years of suffering punishment for breaking Daddy's covenant? You think four years will appease him?

This is an abomination to him. The Jewish people say they have been scattered for 600 years throughout the world. If this is true, out of their own mouth proves they are posers. Our punishment was to last 400 years according to Gen.15:13-14 and Acts 7:6-7 and not a day longer. They are not who they claim to be, Rev. 2:9/Rev. 3:9. They are posers, pretending to be us since they think we lost our covenant rights a long time ago. Their lives are filled with inconsistencies and our stolen history. They made a point of stripping us of our identity in order to promote their fallacies. But they don't know our father. If he's married to the backslider, it should be apparent that he's married to each of his chosen people! We are in a spiritual, intimate relationship with our Heavenly Father. We are his and he is ours!!!! He made sure we would stay in connection with him by hiding Jacob/Israel in the church...even though we are not Christians...we became the church and we still are today!

The most important thing that happen for us was when God gave Jesus to us as a way to redeem us back to him. According to the Cave of Treasures, God promised Adam he would redeem him from his fall of Satan and take back the keys to the kingdom that he stole. Adam made Seth promise that Noah would take his body with him when the flood came. He was to bury Adam's body on Golgotha where Jesus would be crucified. At the time of Jesus crucifixion, a Roman spear pierced his side and water fell to the ground. It went down into the grave and baptized Adam redeeming him from the curse of sin and death and the grave. This is how God redeemed the first man Adam. The descendants of Abraham, Isaac, and Jacob will walk into our promised inheritance. We are the descendants of Jacob. We are the inheritors of the Kingdom of God. This knowledge should make you get up and do a happy dance... our time of bondage is coming to an end in 2019 which will fulfill the 400-year punishment and curse we had to endure.

Conclusion

I have painted a picture of the grand scheme of things. How it permeates our lives. The choice to believe is truly yours with knowledge and understanding of what was done to us. That old system of pagan worship has been sewn into the fabric of our daily lives. Our spiritual light is gone; we are in spiritual darkness without a clue of what is happening to us, Isa 8:22. We unknowingly participate in idol worship when we go to church on Sunday. When we celebrate Christian holidays like Easter and Christmas, we are celebrating the pagan side of these holidays when we participate in buying gifts, new clothes, and in Easter egg hunts. We worship on a Sunday in respect to the Sun God. Sunday is his day of rest. His name is Apollo or Jupiter, the God of Rome and of this world; who is really Satan. Hebrew people are to worship and rest on the Sabbath which is Saturday not Sunday. Esau/Rome created laws that eliminated Sabbath worship. We were killed when our ancestors were caught observing Sabbath or keeping any parts of God's laws.

I have shown you why Esau is trying to destroy our pineal gland. They think by poisoning us with fluoride in our drinking water/toothpaste, they can stop our pineal gland from working. But nothing can separate us from the love of our father. The enemy doesn't know our father who is jealous for us. He will kill for us because we are his. After all of their master plans, disguises, and deceit; they still can't stop what our Father has designed for us. They can't take our place or keep us from going back to our homeland to claim our inheritance, Joel 3:6-7.

Slavery lasted about 246 years. Our adversities of being black in America will last 154 years. This thing has a set time to end. Time started counting towards fulfillment of the curses of 400 years in 1619. At the time of this writing, we have less than 17 months left on the curse/punishment of Deut. 28:15-68. We will experience redemption from the curse and Jubilee in 2019 from our captivity. It will be a release and COMPLETION OF THE CURSE/PUNISHMENT. The curse will be fulfilled, and we will go back to our homeland in Jerusalem, Gen. 15:13-14/Acts 7:6-7. Gentile rule will come to an end when our time of release is come. I am so excited! We are not Christians or Gentiles. We are Hebrew people from Israel who are aliens, a peculiar people, sojourning in a land not our own, 1 Peter 2:9, 11-12. We are God's first family and the elite people of the universe. We are the Twelve Tribes of Israel here in the Americas and scattered to the four corners of the earth, Daughters of Zion, and Sons of God. We are not like other people. There is something special about us. That is why it is said of our women that we have black girl magic. Our people have skills, talent, and athletic prowess that supersede other nations of people.

We have the same weapon that Jesus will use to destroy the wicked from off the earth at his return. We have the "Sword of the Spirit" in our mouths like him, and a river of living water flowing through our bellies. Now is the time to speak things into existence. To declare a thing and see it come to past. Those of us who went church have been trained for such a time as this. We are the first line of defense in the earth. We are spiritual warfare warriors like Jesus. The Ancient of Days claims us as his children and he's coming back for us; I'm glowing, exhilarated, and excited! I am finally complete in him! We are his and he is ours! We are royalty; we are a part of his angelic family who looks just like us in skin complexion and hair. Did you know when we talk down about one another we are talking about God? When we call each other out of our names we are calling God out of his name? Since we have been exiled out of the land, God's name continues to be defiled. When people see us, most refer to us in derogatory names. His name is on us! We must be mindful of this and find love and respect for one another. After all, we are the same family; all twelve tribes! We are the first family of the earth and Jesus is the first fruit from among us!

Let's get ourselves together to get ready to go. Not all of us are going to make it. Some of us Hebrew people want to stay right where they are doing what they do. They are comfortable in their mess. Rev 18:4 says to 'come out of her so we won't be in the way to receive the same punishments that's meant for the world. We are coming out of 'God's Day of Vengeance' while the world will receive their day of visitation. We will become the head again and they will become the tail. Who can stop it? It has been written and so ordained to happen!

There will be a mass migration where we will go back to our homeland. This type of migration happened when we were taken into slavery. The nations will return to their homelands as the world stage is set for the big war that is at hand. The third world war will include a heavenly war because again, Esau is trying to annihilate Jacob as it was in the beginning. We are innocent; we have done nothing to anyone. Our exile is family business. We are being punished by our heavenly father, but Esau continues to put bondages on us and kill us. We are the righteous generation because we did nothing to ayone else; our punishment is between us and God, not the world! They have no right to discipline us because of it, which is why God is wroth. He did not ask man to treat us this way with bondages and atrocities. They are not the executioners of our punishment. We are the last generation to experience Satan's rule in the earth through the Gentiles.

The world is not prepared for what is coming to it. It will be a surreal experience for everyone. Satan and his serpent/reptile people, the fallen angels, Esau and the people of the earth that is with him will war against Daddy Yahweh Sabaoth, The Most Highest God, Jesus, and the Warrior Angelic hosts. God will be fighting for the remnant of his children while protecting us during this great and terrible war, so we won't be wiped out. We will be a part of this great battle either on our heavenly father's side or Satan's side, there is no in between. We are spirit beings having a natural experience in these earth-suits we call a body.

When we die, we go back to our spirit form. Our spirit can never die. There are demonic spirit beings we are trained to war against through our teachings in the Word of God. These spirit beings are real.

Trees of Righteousness/Fulfillment of the Curses of Deuteronomy 28

The bible says the end times will be just like it was in the days of Noah, Luke 17:26. Giants will come back into the earth again.

Alien life has been found in Antarctica encased in an iceberg. These are the captains of the fallen angels. I believe that when we are revealed, these fallen angels will be unleashed. They will be here to torment the ungodly people and for the end time battle of Armageddon. This thing goes deep like a rabbit hole. Our heavenly Father says his people perish for a lack of knowledge, Hosea 4:6. We are Kings/Priests… Emperors/Empresses… royal people…people of the light…Kingdom people, the first family of the earth. His kingdom come, his will be done, on earth as it is in heaven.

We will rule and reign under Jesus our righteous king!

Again, the world's day of vengeance is not meant for us; but if you are attached to this world and the world system, you will receive her punishments! In Malachi 1:3-4, Yahweh Sabaoth says he hates Esau and laid his mountains and heritage waste for the dragons of the wilderness. Edom/Rome says they are impoverished but will return and build the desolate places. God said they will build but he will throw down, and they shall call them 'The borders of wickedness' and the people against whom the Lord hath indignation forever. And your eyes shall see, and ye shall say, The Lord will be magnified from the border of Israel hence, massive hurricanes, violent tornadoes, volcanoes, tsunamis, earthquakes, and the like. This is the first time in history that we have had three cat 4/5 hurricanes with a fourth one threatening to the New England coast and two earthquakes back to back that hit Mexico within a two-week period in the months of August and September 2017.

Daddy God said he would visit the earth with a show of his power against the wicked before he brings us out of all the places, he scattered us, Gen. 15:13-14. Yahweh Sabaoth says he is in the Whirlwind, Nahum 1:2-3. When you think in your heart about the people who lost their lives, please think on this; he allows the rain to fall and the sun to shine on the just and the unjust, so as it is in these natural disasters. All people are affected. He has sealed the 144,000 in our foreheads with an activated pineal gland that will light us up at the designated time in 2019 which is the year of our Jubilee. Freedom from being exiled from our homeland!

He said for me to tell everyone to wear our hair and skin as a badge of honor because, we are the only people like us on the face of the planet. We light up yall like the pictures of God, Jesus, The Saints, and the angels I have provided in this book. The Gentiles think they can erase President Obama's legacy. What they refuse to accept is that President Obama is a foreshadow of things to come. Gentile rule is at its end all over the world. There is nothing they can do to maintain control. The decree has been set. The Lord's Day of Vengeance will come upon them as foretold throughout scripture the very same way it came upon us Israel. I bring a charge of Identity Theft against the nations of the world who participated in the Transatlantic Slave Trade. Everything the nations stole from us must be returned. My heavenly father gave it to us the seed of Abraham, Isaac, and Jacob.

The Thousand Years

The Hebrew year 5779 is a year of being birthed into a nation and war with Satan. A shift has happened in the earth. My logo is prophetic because it pictures a woman with a baby and God's hands holding them up on the continent of Africa with the Middle East added back on to it. A nation being birthed. The baby symbolizes Israel being snatched up to God to be protected so our nation can come forth. The woman is the Mother who facilitates an end time message of our identity. We come from the Middle East which is really Africa, that Esau tried to remove from the continent of Africa Joel 3:2. Daddy God said they parted his land and divided it up as spoil, Joel 3:7 Daddy says he is summoning us back to him. Daddy said, enough of this, tell the nations to prepare for war, Joel 3:9. The same shift that was here 400 years ago that gave our power, wealth, and authority away and sent us into a punishment of a 400-year curse is back again.

We must remember that we are spirit beings inhabiting a flesh body having a natural experience. All of this is spiritual. It is here to transfer what was stolen and taken from us back into our hands. It is time for change because the 400 years are completing. There are specific things that will happen where the world will know who we are when we are revealed. A change of the guard is now taking affect. Africans of the Diaspora rises as a nation preparing for Jesus return to reign in the Kingdom of Righteousness, Isa. 66:8/Rev. 12

Forget reparations, we are getting it all back! I decree and declare that what was taken from Shem be restored to Jacob/Israel in Jesus name...this will fulfill Isa. 60:5. We are in Eze. 37, where we will be revealed as God's children, and all disputes as to who and whose we are will be put to rest. It is now time for black ruler ship again, just as it was from the beginning in Afro-Eurasia. It was the beginning of civilization and the first inhabited land mass that included Africa, Europe, and Asia. It was also known as the Ecumene. A Greek terminology meaning inhabited world.

We are killed for nothing all the daylong! If we are not killing ourselves, then the police and the rest of the Gentiles are taking us out without accountability! No punishment, while the Police still get administrative pay and protection by their Union.

All churches are under the Admiralty Maritime laws. They are designated 501c3 corps and must uphold the teachings of this present world system. Their teachings have us believing we are Christians and Gentiles which is not true. We are Hebrew, and we must separate ourselves from these falsehoods. The Hebrew and the church who have received Jesus as Lord and Savior are excluded from this Day of vengeance our father has planned for the world. Expect to receive your inheritance that has been laid up for you. The wealth of the wicked is laid up for the righteous...we are the righteous generation! We shall come into our Jubilee and inheritance Abba Yahweh, The Ancient One has in store for us. If he be for us, who could be against us! Your Abba says do not be afraid of them, for he himself will fight for you, Deut. 3:22. When we go into the land this time...our father says we will not ever have to worry about the oppressor again. He will remove them far away from us. We will never be a laughingstock to the nations again, Joel 2:19.

Our Father wants to show us his power, strength, and protection for his children. We are his children. He is wroth with the world for their mistreatment of us; his Holy people and their refusal to accept him as their God and Creator. He has made us the world's blessing! We are going back to a time when Adam and his family all the way down to his descendant Noah, would go to the Mountain of God with the Angels and sing praise and worship to our Abba Yahweh, "The Book of the Cave of Treasures". I have included pictures of treasures of darkness and hidden riches of secret places that you may know that I, the Lord, which call you by your name, am the God of Israel, Isa. 45:3. It is now time for black rulership again, just as it was from the beginning in Afro-Eurasia. It was the beginning of civilization and the first inhabited land mass that included Africa, Europe, and Asia. It was also known as the Ecumene. A Greek terminology meaning inhabited world.

We are going through the testings and trials of Job. God allowed Satan to have his time in the earth to collect all those souls that do not love God or his children. This was Satan's designated time to rule as God of this world and then his eventual fall. He is a defeated, demonic foe that we keep subdued under our feet.

Revelation 20:1-15

1 And I saw an angel coming down out of heaven, having the key to

the Abyss and holding in his hand a great chain. 2 He seized the dragon, that ancient serpent, who is the devil, or Satan, and bound him for a thousand years. 3 He threw him into the Abyss, and locked and sealed it over him, to keep him from deceiving the nations anymore until the thousand years were ended. After that, he must be set free for a short time. 4 I saw thrones on which were seated those who had been given authority to judge. And I saw the souls of those who had been beheaded because of their testimony about Jesus and because of the word of God. They[a] had not worshiped the beast or its image and had not received its mark on their foreheads or their hands. They came to life and reigned with Christ a thousand years. 5 (The rest of the dead did not come to life until the thousand years were ended.) This is the first resurrection. 6 Blessed and holy are those who share in the first resurrection. The second death has no power over them, but they will be priests of God and of Christ and will reign with him for a thousand years.

The Judgment of Satan

7 When the thousand years are over, Satan will be released from his prison 8 and will go out to deceive the nations in the four corners of the earth—Gog and Magog—and to gather them for battle. In number they are like the sand on the seashore. 9 They marched across the breadth of the earth and surrounded the camp of God's people, the city he loves. But fire came down from heaven and devoured them. 10 And the devil, who deceived them, was thrown into the lake of burning sulfur, where the beast and the false prophet had been thrown.

They will be tormented day and night for ever and ever.

The Judgment of the Dead

11 Then I saw a great white throne and him who was seated on it. The earth and the heavens fled from his presence, and there was no place for them. 12 And I saw the dead, great and small, standing before the throne, and books were opened. Another book was opened, which is the book of life. The dead were judged according to what they had done as recorded in the books. 13 The sea gave up the dead that were in it, and death and Hades gave up the dead that were in them, and each person was judged according to what they had done. 14 Then death and Hades were thrown into the lake of fire. The lake of fire is the second death. 15 Anyone whose name was not found written in the book of life was thrown into the lake of fire.

I bring a charge of Identity Theft against the nations of the world who participated in the Transatlantic Slave Trade. Everything the nations stole from us must be returned. My heavenly father gave it to us the seed of Abraham, Isaac, and Jacob as our inheritance. Our Father wants to show us his power, strength, and protection for his children. We are his children. He is wroth with the world for their mistreatment of us; his Holy people and their refusal to accept him as their God and Creator. He has made us the world's blessing! We are going back to a time when Adam and his family all the way down to his descendant Noah, would go to the Mountain of God with the Angels and sing praise and worship to our Abba Yahweh, "The Book of the Cave of Treasures". I have included pictures of treasures of darkness and hidden riches of secret places that you may know that I, the Lord, which call you by your name, am the God of Israel, Isa. 45:3.

Photocopies of Historic Artwork

Most of these pictures have been lightened or 'whitenized' to promote a lie of our stolen history.

I have a righteous indignation!

Empress Em Sharon Yisrael

Yahweh Sabaoth, the God of War...Daddy God

This picture has been whitened...they forgot his foot...and his hair is in locks!!!

Figure Figure * ARABIC 3 Blake, Williams "Ancient of Days" 1794

Empress Em Sharon Yisrael

Figure 2 "Stories of The Saints" Unknown

Figure 1 Albi Cathedral "The Expulsion of Adam and Eve From Pardise" Unknown

Trees of Righteousness/Fulfillment of the Curses of Deuteronomy 28

Figure 3 "Saint George The Victorious" Unknown

Figure 4 "The Calling of The Apostles" Unknown

Figure 5 "Saint Marina of Antioch" Unknown

Figure 6 "Russian Icon of Saint George" Unknown

Trees of Righteousness/Fulfillment of the Curses of Deuteronomy 28

Figure 8 "Saint George The Victorious" Unknown

Figure 7 "Expulsion of The Dragon by Archangel Gabriel" Unknown

Figure 10 Daineko, "Apocalypse - Fair Judge" Unknown

Figure 9 Reublev, Andrei "Holy Trinity" 1400

Figure 12 "Archangel Gabriel" Unknown

Figure 11 "Saint Michael the Archangel" Unknown

Figure 14 "Immanuel Icon" Unknown

Figure 13 "Archangel Michael" Orthodox Church, Unknown

Trees of Righteousness/Fulfillment of the Curses of Deuteronomy 28

Figure 16 "Taxisarchis and Archangel Michael" Unknown

Figure 15 Icon Synaxis of Archangels, Unknown

Figure 17 Archangels, Unown

Figure 19 "Ustyug Annunciation" Russian Icon, 1140

Figure 18 Theopan Greek Transfiguration, Russian Icon

Figure 21 St. Michael, Orhtodox Church Icon, Unknown

Figure 20 Rublev, Andrei "Archangel Gabriel" 1360-1430

Trees of Righteousness/Fulfillment of the Curses of Deuteronomy 28

Figure 15 Icon Synaxis of Archangels, Unknown

Figure 16 "Taxisarchis and Archangel Michael" Unknown

Figure 17 Archangels, Unown

Figure 19 "Ustyug Annunciation" Russian Icon, 1140

Figure 18 Theopan Greek Transfiguration, Russian Icon

Figure 21 St. Michael, Orhtodox Church Icon, Unknown

Figure 20 Rublev, Andrei "Archangel Gabriel" 1360-1430

Trees of Righteousness/Fulfillment of the Curses of Deuteronomy 28

Figure 22 Icon St. George the Martyr, Unknown

Figure 23 "The Transfiguration" Unknown

Figure 26 Holy Trinity Icon

Figure 25 Archangel Icon, Unknown

Figure 24 Sunday of The Last Judgement, Unknown

Trees of Righteousness/Fulfillment of the Curses of Deuteronomy 28

Figure 27 Last Judgement of The Lord, Icon

Figure 29 Ladder of Divine Descent, from Monastary of St. Catherine

Figure 28 Russian Icon of Three Holy Hierarchs, 1830

Figure 31 St Basil The Great, Unknown

Figure 30 Invocation of Saint Blaise, Unknown

Figure 32 Blessed John The Hairy, Unknown

Figure 33 St. Clement of Alexandria, Unknown

Trees of Righteousness/Fulfillment of the Curses of Deuteronomy 28

Figure 34 St. Nicholas the Miracle Worker, 16 Century

Figure 35 Moses with The 10 Commandments, Unknown

Pope Clement I - After the death of the Apostle Peter, St. Linus (67-79) was the next Bishop of Rome, succeeded by St. Anacletus (79-91), and then St. Clement (92-101)

Figure 36 Pope Clement I, Unknown

Figure 37 St. Nicholas, Unknown

Trees of Righteousness/Fulfillment of the Curses of Deuteronomy 28

Figure 39 St. Nicholas Icon

Figure 38 St Moses the Black, Icon

Figure 40 Sava The Abbot, unknown

Figure 41 Icon "Saint Moses The Black" unknown

Trees of Righteousness/Fulfillment of the Curses of Deuteronomy 28

Saint Clement is said to have known St. Peter, St. Luke, Barnabas and even St. Paul personally, and he even traveled with them on several occasions. After St. Peter and his first two successors, Linus and Cletus were martyred, he was appointed Bishop of Rome and the 3rd successor of Saint Peter (The 4th Pope).

Figure 43 Russian Orthodox Icon, Saint Clement

Figure 42 St James The Just, Catholic Icon,

Cretan Byzantine icon by the hand of Angelos, circa 1400. It is kept at Saint Catherine's Monastery at Mount Sinai. It depicts St. John the Evangelist dictating his Gospel to his disciple St. Prochorus.

Figure 44 Saint John the Evangelist, Icon

Trees of Righteousness/Fulfillment of the Curses of Deuteronomy 28

Figure 45 St. Cybi and St. Seiriol

Apostle Nicanor the Deacon of the Seventy. In the Acts of the Holy Apostles (6: 1-6) it is said that the twelve Apostles chose seven men: Stephen, Philip, Prochorus, Nicanor, Timon, Parmenas and Nicholas, full of the Holy Spirit and wisdom, and established them to serve as deacons.

Figure 46 Apostle Nicanor The Deacon of the Seventy, Unknown

The Conception by Righteous Anna of the Most Holy Mother of God. St. Anna, the mother of the Virgin Mary, was the youngest daughter of the priest Nathan from Bethlehem, descended from the tribe of Levi. She married St. Joachim, who was a native of Galilee.

Figure 47 The Conception By Righteous Anna, Unknown

Trees of Righteousness/Fulfillment of the Curses of Deuteronomy 28

Saint Catherine Invested with the Dominican Habit, by Giovanni di Paolo (1461)

Figure 48 DiPaolo, Giovanni "Saint Catherine Invested with the Dominican Habit" 1461

St. Peter the Metropolitan of Moscow and Wonderworker of All Russia, died 1326.

Figure 49 Saint Peter The Metropolitan of Moscow, Unknown

Trees of Righteousness/Fulfillment of the Curses of Deuteronomy 28

Peter I, King of Bulgaria, son of Simeon I of Bulgaria, died 970

Figure 50 Peter the I, King of Bulgaria, Unknown

Saint Sophia Cathedral in Novgorod Russia icon

Figure 51 John Climacus, George, and Vlasius, Russian Icon

King Stephen Uros III (Decanski) of Serbia, died 1331. Icon given to the Basilica di San Nicola, Bari, Italy by King Stephen Decani and his wife in 1327, in gratitude for the king's restored sight
Postcard: Basilica di San Nicola, Bari, Italy

Figure 52 King Stephen Uros III, Icon

St. Theodore the Archbishop of Rostov, died 1394.

Figure 53 St. Theodore the Archbishop of Rostov, Icon

Trees of Righteousness/Fulfillment of the Curses of Deuteronomy 28

Figure 55 St. Benedict the African

Figure 54 The Raising of Lazarus, Icon

Figure 56 Papas, Nichols "The Confessing Baptist" Unknown

Figure 57 Saint Eudokia Martyr of Heliopolis, Unknown

Trees of Righteousness/Fulfillment of the Curses of Deuteronomy 28

From: The Secret Book of Honour of the Fugger family of Kirchberg and Weissenhorn. Paintings by Jörg Breu the Younger. Augsburg, 1545-1549 with supplements 16-19th Century. A Google translation yields the woman with the hat (not the Queen) as the Matriarch Ursula von Harrach (1522-1554).

Figure 58 Jorg Breu the Younger, "Fugger Family of Kirckberg and Weissenhorn" 16th - 19th Century

Empress Em Sharon Yisrael

Marquess of Hertford Coat of Arms, with two Roman Soldier supporters. (Note stylized Roman uniforms).

Figure 59 Marquess of Herford Coat of Arms, Unknown

Trees of Righteousness/Fulfillment of the Curses of Deuteronomy 28

Figure 60 Arms of Silas Titus of Bushey, 1623-1704

Figure 61 Ana Nzinga Queen of Angola, Unknown

Yates Thompson 37 f. 86 - Miniature of a group of saints, including a bearded pope, two bishops, a king with a book, Peter and Benedict, at the beginning of the reading for All Saints, in the Hours of the Virgin. Origin: France, Central (Paris and Bourges) c. 1405-1410 A.D.

Figure 63 Yates Thompson, Miniatur of a Group of Saints, 1405-1410

Figure 62 Limbourg Brothers, "Labor Of The Month Tiles" 1412

Trees of Righteousness/Fulfillment of the Curses of Deuteronomy 28

Detail of a miniature of a woman before a man seated on a throne, with two men seated behind her, in 'Le Débat du livre des ii amans'.

Figure 64 "St George", Unknown

Miniature of three pairs of lovers being presented to Jean de Werchin, Seneschal of Hainault (Belgium), in 'Le Livre des iii jugements'. circa 1410

Figure 65 Jean de Werchin, 1410

Figure 66 Swabian War 1499, Unknown

Figure 67 Swabian War 1499, unknown

Figure 68 Swabian War 1499, Unknown

Figure 69 Swabian War 1499, Unknown

Figure 70 Marteen De Vos "The Adoration of the Magi" 1599

Figure 71 Richard II, Unknown

Trees of Righteousness/Fulfillment of the Curses of Deuteronomy 28

King Boris I of Bulgaria, also known as Boris-Mihail (Michael) died 2 May 907) was the Knyaz (Prince) of First Bulgarian Empire in 852–889. At the time of his baptism in 864, Boris was named Michael after his godfather, Byzantine Emperor Michael III.

Figure 72 King Boris of Bulgaria, Unknown

Figure 73 Richard II of England, Unknown

Figure 74 Master of Alkmaar, "Adoration of the Magi" 1500-1504

Trees of Righteousness/Fulfillment of the Curses of Deuteronomy 28

Figure 76 Jacob Cornelisz Van Oostsanen "Adoration of The Magi" 1510

Figure 75 Religious Icon, Unknown

Figure 77 Unknown Coat of Arms

Empress Em Sharon Yisrael

Figure 78 King James Coat of Arms, Unknown

Figure 79 Saint Maurice and Benedictine Pope, 1420-1430

Trees of Righteousness/Fulfillment of the Curses of Deuteronomy 28

Figure 80 Emperor Yohannes Mural From Athbeha Church, Unknown

Figure 81 King David Russian Icon, Unknown

Figure 82 Wall Painting of Temple Beit Al Wali Nubia, Unknown

Figure 83 First Dentist Hesi Re, Egyptian Artifact, Unknown

Trees of Righteousness/Fulfillment of the Curses of Deuteronomy 28

Figure 84 Stone Panel from North Palace of Ashurbanipal, 645 B.C.

Figure 85 Hildesheim, Scene From the Life of Saints, 1170

Figure 86 Hildesheim, Scene From The Life of Saints, 1170

Trees of Righteousness/Fulfillment of the Curses of Deuteronomy 28

Figure 87 Hildesheim, Scene From the Life of Saints, 1170

Figure 88 Hildesheim, Scene From the Life of Saints, 1170

Figure 89 Hildesheim, Scene From The Life of Saints, 1170

Figure 90 Hildesheim, Scene From the LIfe of Saints, 1170

Trees of Righteousness/Fulfillment of the Curses of Deuteronomy 28

Figure 91 Assyrian Relief

Figure 93 Assyrian Relief

Figure 94 18th Century Map of Africa

Table of Figures

Figure 1 Albi Cathedral "The Expulsion of Adam and Eve From Pardise" Unknown 132

Figure 2 "Stories of The Saints" Unknown 132

Figure 3 "Saint George The Victorious" Unknown 133

Figure 4 "The Calling of The Apostles" Unknown 133

Figure 5 "Saint Marina of Antioch" Unknown 134

Figure 6 "Russian Icon of Saint George" Unknown 134

Figure 7 "Expulsion of The Dragon by Archangel Gabriel" Unknown 135

Figure 8 "Saint George The Victorious" Unknown 135

Figure 9 Reublev, Andrei "Holy Trinity" 1400 135

Figure 10 Daineko, "Apocalypse – Fair Judge" Unknown 135

Figure 11 "Saint Michael the Archangel" Unknown 136

Figure 12 "Archangel Gabriel" Unknown 136

Figure 13 "Archangel Michael" Orthodox Church, Unknown 136

Figure 14 "Immanuel Icon" Unknown 136

Figure 15 Icon Synaxis of Archangels, Unknown 137

Figure 16 "Taxisarchis and Archangel Michael" Unknown 137

Figure 17 Archangels, Unown 137

Figure 18 Theopan Greek Transfiguration, Russian Icon 138

Figure 19 "Ustyug Annunciation" Russian Icon, 1140 138

Figure 20 Rublev, Andrei "Archangel Gabriel" 1360-1430 138

Figure 21 St. Michael, Orhtodox Church Icon, Unknown 138

Figure 22 Icon St. George the Martyr, Unknown 139

Figure 23 "The Transfiguration" Unknown 139

Figure 24 Sunday of The Last Judgement, Unknown 140

Figure 25 Archangel Icon, Unknown 140

Figure 26 Holy Trinity Icon 140

Figure 27 Last Judgement of The Lord, Icon 141

Figure 28 Russian Icon of Three Holy Hierarchs, 1830 142

Figure 29 Ladder of Divine Descent, from Monastary of St. Catherine 142

Figure 30 Invocation of Saint Blaise, Unknown 143

Figure 31 St Basil The Great, Unknown 143

Figure 32 Blessed John The Hairy, Unknown 144

Figure 33 St. Clement of Alexandria, Unknown 144

Figure 34 St. Nicholas the Miracle Worker, 16 Century 145

Figure 35 Moses with The 10 Commandments, Unknown 145

Figure 36 Pope Clement I, Unknown 146

Figure 37 St. Nicholas, Unknown 146

Figure 38 St Moses the Black, Icon 147

Figure 39 St. Nicholas Icon 147

Figure 40 Sava The Abbot, unknown 147

Figure 41 Icon "Saint Moses The Black" unknown 148

Figure 42 St James The Just, Catholic Icon, ...149

Figure 43 Russian Orthodox Icon, Saint Clement 149

Figure 44 Saint John the Evangelist, Icon 150

Figure 45 St. Cybi and St. Seiriol 151

Figure 46 Apostle Nicanor The Deacon of the Seventy, Unknown 151

Figure 47 The Conception By Righteous Anna, Unknown 152

Figure 48 DiPaolo, Giovanni "Saint Catherine Invested with the Dominican Habit" 1461 153

Figure 49 Saint Peter The Metropolitan of Moscow, Unknown 154

Figure 50 Peter the I, King of Bulgaria, Unknown 155

Figure 51 John Climacus, George, and Vlasius, Russian Icon 155

Figure 52 King Stephen Uros III, Icon 156

Figure 53 St. Theodore the Archbishop of Rostov, Icon 156

Figure 54 The Raising of Lazarus, Icon 157

Figure 55 St. Benedict the African 157

Figure 56 Papas, Nichols "The Confessing Baptist" Unknown 157

Figure 57 Saint Eudokia Martyr of Heliopolis, Unknown 158

Figure 58 Jorg Breu the Younger, "Fugger Family of Kirckberg and Weissenhorn" 16th - 19th Century 159

Figure 59 Marquess of Herford Coat of Arms, Unknown 160

Figure 60 Arms of Silas Titus of Bushey, 1623-1704 161

Figure 61 Ana Nzinga Queen of Angola, Unknown 161

Figure 62 Limbourg Brothers, "Labor Of The Month Tiles" 1412 162

Figure 63 Yates Thompson, Miniatur of a Group of Saints, 1405-1410 162

Figure 64 "St George", Unknown 163

Figure 65 Jean de Werchin, 1410 163

Figure 66 Swabian War 1499, Unknown 164

Figure 67 Swabian War 1499, unknown 164

Figure 68 Swabian War 1499, Unknown 165

Figure 69 Swabian War 1499, Unknown 165

Figure 70 Marteen De Vos "The Adoration of the Magi" 1599 166

Figure 71 Richard II, Unknown 166

Figure 72 King Boris of Bulgaria, Unknown 167

Figure 73 Richard II of England, Unknown 167

Figure 74 Master of Alkmaar, "Adoration of the Magi" 1500-1504 168

Figure 75 Religious Icon, Unknown 169

Figure 76 Jacob Cornelisz Van Oostsanen "Adoration of The Magi" 1510 169

Figure 77 Unknown Coat of Arms 169

Figure 78 King James Coat of Arms, Unknown 170

Figure 79 Saint Maurice and Benedictine Pope, 1420-1430 170

Figure 80 Emperor Yohannes Mural From Athbeha Church, Unknown 171

Figure 81 King David Russian Icon, Unknown 171

Figure 82 Wall Painting of Temple Beit Al Wali Nubia, Unknown 172

Figure 83 First Dentist Hesi Re, Egyptian Artifact, Unknown 172

Figure 84 Stone Panel from North Palace of Ashurbanipal, 645 B.C. 173

Figure 85 Hildesheim, Scene From the Life of Saints, 1170 174

Figure 86 Hildesheim, Scene From The Life of Saints, 1170 174

Figure 87 Hildesheim, Scene From the Life of Saints, 1170 175

Figure 88 Hildesheim, Scene From the Life of Saints, 1170 175

Figure 89 Hildesheim, Scene From The Life of Saints, 1170 176

Figure 90 Hildesheim, Scene From the LIfe of Saints, 1170 176

Figure 91 Assyrian Relief 177

Figure 92 Assyrian Relief Hebrew Captivity 177

Figure 93 Assyrian Relief 177

Figure 94 18th Century Map of Africa 178

www.ingramcontent.com/pod-product-compliance
Lightning Source LLC
Chambersburg PA
CBHW051405070526
44584CB00023B/3307